THE GATES OF NIRVANA'S PIT

DRAWN FROM REAL-
LIFE EVENTS

BY

CORTNEY PAGE

DEDICATION

To Dina, Tonya, and Kurt Fenstad,

With love and gratitude for your unwavering support and inspiration. You've been the wind beneath my wings, my guiding stars. Thank you for believing in me and lighting up my path.

Always,

Cortney Page

Table of Contents

PREFACE

What you are about to read is my story, a journey filled with unexpected twists and turns. My name is Cortney Page, and my life has been anything but ordinary. Crossing paths with Bill Gates led to a series of unforgettable and intense encounters. From secret meetings in luxurious settings like the Bellagio Hotel to high-stakes interactions involving influential figures, my life unfolded in ways I could never have imagined.

My interactions with Bill Gates took me through a variety of unexpected settings, from the intimate enclosure of a Jacuzzi to the confined space of an elevator, and even to a public lobby. Each encounter revealed more about the complexities of our bond and the challenges we faced together. My past, intertwined with powerful individuals like Kurt Cobain, Brad Pitt, and Jason Priestley, adds multiple facets to my narrative, highlighting the challenges and choices I faced.

But my story is not just one of passionate encounters and high-profile interactions. It is also a tale marked by deep personal tragedy and resilience. My life took a dark turn when I was assaulted, a trauma that left me with profound emotional scars and fragmented memories. The aftermath of this event reshaped my life, leading to a journey of self-discovery and healing as I struggled to piece together my past and reclaim my identity.

The memory loss that followed the assault introduced another dimension of difficulty to my life. I found myself navigating a world where my past was a series of disjointed images and incomplete stories. This struggle to remember and the pain of what I did recall influenced every aspect of my daily life, from my relationships to my sense of self.

This story delves into my world, exploring my emotions, decisions, and the impact of my relationships. It is a story of passion, intrigue, and the human experience, inviting you to journey alongside me as I live my extraordinary life. From the highs of luxurious adventures to the lows of personal trauma, this book has my story that shows the resilience of the human spirit and the ongoing search for identity and understanding.

Chapter 1
Who is Who?

Looks can be misleading. Only when we dig deeper can we really figure out who's who in this world.

In the lively streets of Los Angeles, Cortney Page, a 24-year-old with an allure reminiscent of Marilyn Monroe, emerges from her luxurious Century City apartment with her Yorkshire Terrier named Gioia nestled in her arms as she steps into her car. Navigating through the bustling streets of Los Angeles, her charming presence captivates passersby, drawing them into the enchanting world she embodies.

Driving her convertible down San Vicente, Cortney passed through Brentwood, a neighborhood once frequented by Marilyn Monroe, feeling the echoes of Hollywood's glamorous past whispering around her. As she cruised past the iconic landmarks, the upbeat melody of Tina Turner's "The Best" resonated in her car, its lyrics fueling her strong desire to be the best.

Amidst the nostalgia and allure of Marilyn's old stomping grounds, Cortney felt a deep sense of belonging. As a Marilyn impersonator herself, she couldn't help but feel like she was at the top of the world. With the wind in her platinum blonde hair and the music in her ears, Cortney embraced the moment, feeling as though she was destined for greatness in the city where dreams are made.

In a lavish Santa Monica condo, Dina Parker, 25, embodied the essence of Marilyn Monroe with stunning resemblance, captivating onlookers with her mysterious aura. She served as a body double in the movie "Marilyn and Me" and also portrayed Monroe in a nighttime beach scene for a TV movie. In contrast, Cortney effortlessly secured speaking roles without auditions. Despite her glamorous life, Dina was also a mother to a three-year-old son with famous skateboarder Steve Olson. Two Marilyn Monroe doppelgängers, their lives intertwined amidst the glitz and glamor of Los Angeles, set on their journey where reality often blurred.

As they rode together in the car, the radio crackled, broadcasting a news report: The Green River killer strikes again in Seattle.

Cortney quickly switched off the radio, and the car fell into tense silence as she continued driving deeper into Hollywood.

"That reminds me, how was your gig at the strip bar with your photographer friend?" Cortney asked with eagerness. This was her trademark: she did everything with an open heart and a fiery spirit, even with the smallest tasks, she'd dive right in.

"It was quite a journey. We drove up there in a van with something like 'Thirteen Ugly Girls and

One Pretty One' painted on the side," Dina replied, her voice hinting exhaustion.

"That's hilarious. Does Paul know I am using the studio to record my songs?" Cortney replied with a chuckle on her face; the title amused her.

"I don't think so, especially since I towed Shirley MacLaine's car so Barbara Streisand could park there. Shirley MacLaine was next door shopping for pillows." Dina responded with her voice remaining monotone.

"Oh my god, Dina, that's totally newsworthy!" Cortney exclaimed, her excitement evident as she visibly jumped in her seat.

"It's really not that big of a deal," Dina replied, her tone reflecting her lack of enthusiasm as she was puzzled by Cortney's excessive excitement, unable to understand why it was such a significant event to her.

Cortney quickly assessed the situation, noticing Dina's expression and sensing her discomfort, she smoothly transitioned to a different topic.

"Thanks for coming tonight and supporting my band and me," said Cortney.

"Sure thing," Dina replied.

Upon hearing Dina's brief response, Cortney recognized that it would be better to change the subject, not wanting to upset Dina any further.

"And, you don't mind holding Gioia for me?" Cortney asked with a consistent smile on her face.

"I don't mind. Jenna and Tonya will help me look after her." Dina replied with a smile; this time, there was a certain warmness in her tone.

"We'll be sitting with Kennedy at his table," Cortney exclaimed, excitement evident once more in her tone.

"Kennedy!" screamed Dina, her voice vivid with shock. She shifted her gaze towards Cortney, who was behind the wheel with a smile adorning her face. Dina began to regard her with an envious glance—a jealousy not of malice but tinged with admiration.

"Kennedy Gordy, better known as Rockwell," Cortney replied.

"Is he going to sign you to Motown?" Dina asked with a curious tone, her fascination growing with each of Cortney's responses during their ongoing conversation. She became increasingly awestruck and intrigued, yearning to uncover whether Cortney was on the brink of landing a substantial contract.

"No, he is pitching me to the Playboy channel on Monday. I'm singing my new song tonight, and I don't think he will like it," Cortney replied.

"Jungle Rumble?" Dina threw her guess.

As Cortney and Dina made their way toward the vibrant lights of the club they were headed to, Cortney subtly hinted at her apprehension regarding the reception of her latest musical creation. She was certain that Kennedy wouldn't like the song at all. Amidst the anticipation of the night ahead, Cortney's enigmatic hints suggested a deeper complexity surrounding her relationship with Kennedy and the potential impact of her new song. As they navigated through the bustling streets of Hollywood, the air thick with excitement and uncertainty, Cortney's unspoken fears added an extra layer of intrigue for Dina.

"Yep, here we are... the Pure Platinum Club! You know what?" As they arrived at the club, Cortney remarked, a subtle yet palpable excitement threading through her words. Despite the usual happiness radiating from her, her heart raced with its customary fervor. She embraced her life wholeheartedly, reveling in its current state, her words spilling forth in a rush of excitement.

"What?" Dina curiously asked.

"Never mind," replied Cortney.

Just outside the Pure Platinum Club, the Boulevard buzzed with activity as sleek cars glided along its thoroughfare while throngs of people queued up, their anticipation palpable in the air. Among them stood Jenna King, aged 24, a striking

Madonna impersonator exuding the iconic star's timeless charm, and Tonya Muhlhauser, aged 27, a statuesque redhead, her presence commanding attention in the bustling crowd.

Both of the sparkling ladies were busy chatting as they stood in the line heading to the club entry.

"Did Cortney tell you that I was the one who suggested she play Marilyn Monroe for the Ron Smith Celebrity Lookalikes?" Her words dripped with subtle arrogance as if she believed herself responsible for every success Cortney had ever known.

"She didn't tell me. Ron Smith did," Tonya remarked.

"There they are! Cortney! Dina! Over here!" she exclaimed, pointing with her index finger. Despite the sleek black gloves adorning her hands, the lustrous gleam of her nails shimmered unmistakably, a testament to their impeccable care and attention.

At the forefront of the line, Cortney and Dina conversed with the imposing bouncer, their anticipation palpable in the air. With a graceful gesture, Cortney motioned for Jenna and Tonya, beckoning them to the head of the queue. In a display of camaraderie, they joined forces, striding past the velvet ropes and into the pulsating heart of the club, united in their pursuit of Hollywood's enchantment.

As they stepped in the Pure Platinum Club a vibrant neon sign illuminated the club interior, showcasing "Aldo and the Pharaohs" featuring "Goddess Isis," the girls strolled past with an air of intrigue. Their path led them to the bustling bar, where Rockwell, aged 25, stood poised amidst the crowd of patrons, tall with a sturdy stature that made his sharp suit look even better on him. With a playful grin, Cortney leaned in and gave him a tender kiss on the cheek, catching a whiff of his alluring perfume that only enhanced his charm, igniting a spark of excitement in the electrifying atmosphere of the night.

As Cortney bestowed her affectionate gesture upon Rockwell, a ripple of emotions swept through the group of girls accompanying her. Some regarded her with envious glances, their envy tinged with bitterness, while others gazed upon her with genuine admiration and appreciation for her boldness. Yet, amidst the varying reactions, a subtle tension lingered in the air, casting a shadow over the once-lively atmosphere.

The envious glances from some people threatened to spoil the close bond among the friends as their hidden resentment brewed silently. Meanwhile, those who admired Cortney's confidence and charm felt torn between admiration and envy, uncertain about how to handle the changing dynamics.

Cortney introduced her friends with a soft

tone, gesturing to each one as she spoke. Her face beamed with a radiant smile, reflecting the sincere joy that lit up the room. Her expression exuded warmth and honesty, revealing her pure intentions. There was no hint of ill will in her eyes, only a genuine desire for everyone's happiness.

Surrounded by friends and acquaintances, Cortney's genuineness radiated, effortlessly attracting others to her. She had a natural talent for spreading positivity and brightness, effortlessly uplifting the spirits of those nearby, it was evident that Cortney's heart brimmed with kindness and a sincere desire for everyone's well-being.

"Rockwell, pleased to meet you all," Rockwell nodded with a touch of grace, his actions reflecting his gentlemanly nature. A genuine smile lit up his face, highlighting his charm and sincerity. From the sparkle in his eyes to his confident yet gentle demeanor, it was clear that Rockwell epitomized chivalry and refinement. There was an undeniable magnetism about him that drew others in, leaving no doubt that he was a true gentleman in every sense of the word.

As Jenna, Tonya, Dina, and the adorable dog headed to the bathroom, Cortney saw her chance and acted on it. With determination and grace, she approached Rockwell, her heart racing with anticipation. With a subtle gesture, she passed him her tape, a physical representation of her musical aspirations and dreams.

Since the beginning, she fearlessly pursued opportunities and followed her passions, undeterred by crowds or emotions swirling around her. When Rockwell accepted the tape, it marked their silent agreement of potential and possibility, hanging palpably in the air.

"Here are my tracks. I really appreciate you having me perform tonight," Cortney said with a smile.

"Tonight, we have A&R here, so if Playboy doesn't work out, we'll get you signed with a label." Rockwell assured, his tone steady as his face retained its composed demeanor.

***

Meanwhile, as Jenna excused herself to use the restroom, she heard whispers and the sound of toilets flushing. In one stall, two women were snorting coke. Curiously she knocked on the stall door, and it swung open.

"Can I get a bump?" Jenna asked.

"Sure girl. I just got it from a Pharaoh." The girl handed over the powder.

"You mean the band that's playing tonight?" As Jenna handled the white powder, she casually interjected a question to maintain the flow of conversation.

"Yep, the same one. The music is just a cover

for them dealing." The girl voiced her opinion in a sarcastic tone.

"Does Cortney know that?" Tonya jumped into the conversation with concern as she and Dina stepped in.

"I know Cortney gets weed for our recording clients at the studio, but didn't know she could get coke too..." Dina said.

"What recording studio do you work at?" With a keen interest in the subject, the girl posed her question eagerly.

"Groundcontrol in Santa Monica on Montana," Dina responded in monotone.

"We should leave. The music is starting," Tonya wrapped up the discussion, and the three left together.

***

Meanwhile in Seattle, Daryl Fenstad, 29, while in his one-bedroom apartment, noticed the answering machine blinking with three messages. He pushed the button to play them and sat down on his couch with his portable phone. As the first message popped up, Cortney's voice filled the room, vibrant and excited as she discussed plans for her upcoming visit to Seattle.

"Hey bro, it's your sister. I got a gig in Walla Walla but decided to extend my stay in Seattle for the weekend, crashin' at Kurt's place. It'd be awesome to catch up with you. Catch you later!" Cortney's voice overflowed with excitement.

With Cortney's cheerful voice dancing in the air, Daryl dialed a number on the phone, while the muted TV showed news about the Green River killer.

"Hey Kurt, it's your cousin. I just heard from my sister, and she says that she is coming for a visit and staying with you." Daryl said.

Meanwhile, in Kurt Fenstad's cozy Redmond apartment, the dim light stretches shadows as Kurt grabs the phone with a hint of surprise, "Hey Daryl, I didn't think you were talking to me. You thought I was smoking a bigger crack rock?" Kurt Fenstad chuckled.

Over at the Pure Platinum Club, the air buzzed with energy. Aldo and the Pharaohs had just finished their electrifying performance, and the crowd erupted in applause, their cheers were loud and clear through the dimly lit venue. Rocket, a tall and wiry 25-year-old with an edgy vibe, swayed through the crowd, offering something discreetly. One by one, people shook their heads, declining his offer.

Rocket eventually made his way to Dina, who was sitting at a table near the stage. He leaned in and asked, "Do you want a bump?"

"Not interested, anyway, coke is flowing for free in the bathroom. They say they got it from the

Pharaohs." Dina replied as she glanced up at him, her expression cool and detached.

Rocket pointed towards a band member still lingering on stage, as if to validate Dina's claim. She barely acknowledged the gesture, her focus shifting as Cortney, her platinum blonde hair gleaming under the club lights, stepped onto the stage.

Cortney grabbed the microphone with confidence, the room's attention instantly pivoting to her. As the first beats of "Jungle Rumble" played, she began to sing, her voice cutting through the ambient noise of the club.

"...Here in the hood, stopping wars if I could..."

Her performance drew everyone's gaze and made the earlier conversation fade into the background.

"Jungle Rumble" fades in the air providing a hypothetical background music as thrilling events unfold in downtown Seattle where, Kurt Fenstad, 23, his friend Humberto, 45, and Daryl, cruised the streets, searching for a dealer. As they pulled over, a guy standing on the corner jumped into the backseat with Daryl.

"You got the cash for three rocks?" the dealer asked.

Everyone handed money to the dealer. Kurt

Fenstad loaded the crack pipe and passed it to Daryl, who took a hit before handing it to Humberto. Humberto took a drag and then passed the pipe to Kurt Fenstad, who hit it twice.

"I knew you got the bigger rock to take more hits," Daryl said, a hint of accusation in his voice.

"No, we all got the same size rock," Kurt Fenstad replied calmly.

The dealer, pocketing the money, said, "Ok. Thanks, guys. Have a fucking good night."

As he got out of the car, Daryl kicked him in the back, sending the dealer sprawling into the street as Kurt Fenstad sped off. The song "Jungle Rumble" reached its climax and ended, mirroring the chaos of the scene.

Back in his apartment, Daryl felt a pang of guilt. "I'm sorry, cuz. It was weed greed to the 10th degree," he admitted, the remorse clear in his voice.

"It's okay, Daryl" Kurt Fenstad shrugged, giving him a reassuring look.

Back at the Hollywood alley behind the Pure Platinum Club, Aldo, 25, and the Pharaohs were loading up their equipment when Rocket stepped outside.

"You know this club is my territory, and your white girl was singing about you being bloods and dealing drugs," Rocket said, his tone confrontational.

"Maybe she's just racist and singing about smacking your black ass?" Aldo responded with a smirk as tension ran high.

Rocket threw a punch just as sirens and lights flashed, signaling the arrival of the cops, who quickly moved in to break up the fight.

Next morning, the alarm clock blinked at 7:00 AM, its incessant beeping accompanied by the start of a cheerful tune. Cortney, still half-asleep, reached out to hit the snooze button and rolled over, the soft glow of morning light seeping through the curtains. Moments later, the radio sprang to life again, this time playing "Love Shack." Cortney, now more awake, sighed and swung her legs out of bed, signaling the beginning of a new day. With determined steps, she made her way to the bathroom, the sound of running water filled the apartment as she stepped into the shower.

Just a short while later, she came out of the bathroom feeling a bit more relaxed and sat at her dressing table to get ready. As her puppy, Gioia, and kitten, Osiris, ate, Cortney blow-dried her hair while the radio played news.

The Green River killer has struck not only once, not twice, but three times in the last few months. Bodies were found in the river in the Seattle area. The police do not have a suspect.

Cortney was infused in her thoughts as she braided her hair, put on her wig and makeup, while the radio continued.

Also in the news, Sirhan Sirhan reveals he is a Manchurian candidate. He claims to have been under a spell when he assassinated Senator Robert Kennedy, Jr. at the Ambassador Hotel on June 6, 1968... She reenacted Marilyn Monroe's death believing she was the reincarnation of the late icon. Kay Kent, dead from suicide at 25, was found lifeless in her apartment. She had broken up with her rock star boyfriend, Dean Hammond.

Listening to the news, Cortney's eyes lit up with a plan. It was typical of her to narrate her thoughts aloud, a habit she had developed over the years. "That's it," she said to herself, her voice filled with determination. "I'll be Kay Kent and get myself a rock star boyfriend in Seattle." It was just another instance of Cortney vocalizing her plans and aspirations, a quirk that had become second nature to her.

Cortney's Century City apartment building stood tall, a sleek and modern structure amidst the bustling cityscape. Cortney herself, dressed in a white halter dress reminiscent of Marilyn Monroe's timeless glamor, emerged from the building's entrance, Gioia cradled in her arms as she made her way to her car, ready to start her day. She drives her way to a party store, preparing for where she was actually headed and after a small shopping session, she exits the store with a bundle of colorful balloons that she carefully stows in her car, a touch of excitement evident in her movements.

After arriving at the Burbank residential neighborhood, she drives slowly through the streets as if looking for an address, her demeanor focused yet curious. Neighbors leisurely walk their dogs and tend to their lawns, casting friendly glances as Cortney pulls into a driveway.

As she reaches her destination, Cortney steps out of her car, the vibrant balloons adding a playful touch to her ensemble. With a confident stride, she approaches the door of the modest home with a smile on her face. Upon knocking, a man in his 50s, wearing a robe, answers the door with a curious yet intrigued expression. Cortney greets him with a warm smile and holds her handheld microphone, ready to play some music. With a quick movement, she starts the music, filling the air with melodic notes as she confidently enters the home.

She follows the man to his living room, the atmosphere relaxed yet tinged with anticipation. As he settles onto the couch, she begins to sing her song, filling the room with her melodic voice.

"...While teeing off a game of golf, I may make a play for the caddy..."

"Can I play with myself?" the man quipped.

"I don't need an organ for this song." Cortney responded with a playful yet assertive tone.

Exiting the man's house after concluding her visit, Cortney was met with a suggestive catcall whistle from a passing neighbor as she made her way back to her car.

"Throw money," she yelled back with assertiveness in her voice.

Returning to her apartment, Cortney carried Gioia inside, only to be met with a scene of utter chaos. Her heart pounded in her chest as she took in the devastation before her. The pristine space of her home was now a mess, with belongings scattered haphazardly across the floor. Shock washed over her as she saw her sofa, cruelly cut up and its stuffing spilling out like a wound. But it was the sight of the search warrant lying ominously on the dining room table that brought her world crashing down.

She couldn't make sense of what happened and why until the answering machine beeped and Rockwell's voice came through with a clear sense of urgency.

"Aldo and the band are in jail. Rocket started shit last night, and they got into it right in front of the cops. Rocket said you are the kingpin of the operation. I had to give them your address. Call me as soon as you get this message."

Chapter 2
A Bloodshot Eyed Marilyn

In every note, a story; in every chord, a journey.

Cortney's voice echoed through the quietude of her apartment as she called out to her kitten, "Osiris, here kitty, kitty. Osiris. Psst. Psst. Here kitty, kitty." Soon after Osiris came out of hiding and she tended to him.

Cortney's attention shifted to the blinking light of her answering machine. With a mixture of curiosity and trepidation, she pressed play, her heart pounding in anticipation of what she might hear next.

The voice of Rockwell filled the room, his urgent message delivered with a sense of gravity. "Aldo and the band are in jail. Rocket started shit last night and they got into it right in front of the cops. Rocket said you are the kingpin of the operation. I had to give them your address. Call me as soon as you get this message."

Fighting back a surge of panic, Cortney wasted no time. With trembling hands, she reached for the phone and dialed a familiar number, desperate for assistance in navigating the dire predicament she now found herself in.

Meanwhile, in a darkened bedroom elsewhere

in Seattle, Kurt Fenstad stirred from his slumber as the shrill ring of his landline pierced the silence. With bleary eyes, he reached for the receiver, unaware of the tumultuous events unfolding on the other end of the line.

"Hello," he mumbled groggily, his voice heavy with sleep.

"Kurt, it's me. I'm in trouble," came Cortney's urgent voice as she told him about the recent happenings.

***

At the bustling Seattle International Airport, Cortney, dressed as Marilyn Monroe, stood patiently in line at the ticket desk, her small suitcase in tow. As she waited, a murmur of excitement rippled through the crowd, and curious onlookers began to point and whisper amongst themselves.

A teenage boy tapped her on the shoulder, his eyes wide with awe.

"Excuse me, are you famous? Can I get your autograph?" he asked eagerly.

Cortney flashed him a warm smile, her blue eyes twinkling with amusement. "I'm not famous yet, but I'm on my way to becoming famous," she replied confidently.

With a flourish, she signed the teenager's notepad, eliciting a grin of delight from him.

"You look just like Marilyn Monroe," the teenage boy exclaimed in admiration.

Cortney chuckled softly, a hint of mystery dancing in her voice. "You know what?"

"What?" The boy asked.

"Never mind." She replied and with a playful wink, she turned back to the ticket desk, her heart fluttering with anticipation for the journey ahead.

Inside the small commuter plane, Cortney stowed her suitcase in the overhead compartment before settling into her seat beside a woman around 30 years old.

"Hi. I'm Cortney Page. I'm on my way to Walla Walla to open up a Nostrums department store. They will be taking pictures," Cortney introduced herself with a friendly smile.

"I'm Tracy, a stewardess flying to our next spot." The woman introduced herself as a stewardess flying to their next destination.

"I thought this was a direct flight," Cortney remarked with surprise.

Tracy explained, "It is, but when we touch down, I will get off."

Cortney closed her eyes, intending to rest during the flight. However, she was jolted awake when she felt the plane door begin to rattle

THE GATES OF NIRVANA'S PIT

ominously. Startled, she opened her eyes just in time to see Tracy climbing over her to hold the door closed.

"What is happening?" Cortney asked in a shocking tone.

"Nothing, just... the door, it's rattling." Tracy responded, her expression filled with concern. Tracy got up and held the door closed.

Cortney's eyes widened in alarm and as the commuter plane landed and passengers began to disembark, Tracy and a few others exited the plane. Cortney hesitated for a moment before making a decision. With a determined expression, she rose from her seat and followed them off the plane.

Meanwhile, the scene at Walla Walla Airport, where Cortney was originally supposed to arrive, was nothing short of spectacular. Dozens of people stood eagerly on the tarmac, holding bouquets of flowers, their faces lit with anticipation. A marching band was ready to play, their instruments gleaming in the daylight. A sleek limo waited nearby, adding a touch of luxury to the occasion. Amidst this lively setup, a photographer stood poised, camera in hand, ready to capture the moment Cortney's plane touched down but she wasn't on the plane as she had already gotten off.

As she scanned the small airport for a taxi, a car pulled up, and two men stepped out, introducing themselves as Mike and Brian.

"I'm Mike, and this is Brian," Mike said with a friendly grin.

"Hi. Where are you going?" Brian asked.

"Walla Walla," Cortney replied with concern.

"That's miles away," Mike remarked, sounding surprised.

"You've got to be joking. No cabs?" Cortney inquired, her eyebrows furrowing.

"Looks like you got off at the wrong airport," Brian said after observing the situation.

"No. The plane was unsafe. A stewardess had to hold the door close," Cortney explained, revealing her unease.

"Brian and I will drive you to your gig," Mike offered with confidence.

"How did you know I was going for a gig?" Cortney asked as her curiosity piqued.

"Your appearance is big news around these parts. You are Cortney Page, also known as Goddess Isis," Mike replied.

"Let's go," Brian urged, his voice eager.

"You know what?" Cortney interjected, her tone hesitant.

"What?" Mike and Brian responded in unison.

"Never mind."

Cortney handed her suitcase to Mike, and Brian closed the door behind her. As Mike and Brian exchanged high fives before getting into the car, Cortney settled into her seat, unsure of what awaited her on this unexpected journey.

Inside Brian's car, the atmosphere was relaxed. Mike pulled out a joint, lit it, and passed it to Cortney. Pink Floyd's "Shine on You Crazy Diamond" played softly in the background as they drove through expansive farmlands with snow-capped mountains visible in the distance. The journey was peaceful, the scenery picturesque, and the conversation minimal, allowing the music and the moment to dominate their senses.

***

As night fell, they arrived at Nordstrom department store. Cortney stepped out of the car, suitcase in hand, and looked at the long lines of people waiting outside. She walked confidently towards the security guard holding a walkie-talkie.

"Hi, I'm Marilyn Monroe, and I'm here to take pictures with your guests," Cortney said with a smile.

The security guard, surprised but professional, spoke into his walkie-talkie. "Hi, Marilyn Monroe made it and is here to take pictures."

A female voice crackled back, "Tell her to go to the third floor, and I'll take her to the photographer."

Inside the store, Cortney walked up two flights of stairs with her suitcase. The ambiance was bustling, with shoppers and staff moving about. A woman hurried over to her, shook her hand enthusiastically, and led her to the studio area set up for pictures.

"Hi, Marilyn. I heard you had a reputation for being late. Today, I was at the airport to take pictures for the newspaper, and you were a no show," the photographer remarked, a hint of irritation in his voice.

"A pleasure, I'm ever so sure," Cortney replied, maintaining her poise despite her bloodshot eyes from smoking pot.

She then posed with various guests, her practiced smile never wavering. The evening carried on with the flash of cameras and the hum of excitement from the crowd, encapsulating the surreal blend of glamor and the reality of her unconventional journey to this point.

After successfully ending her gig, Cortney walked down the dimly lit hallway of the hotel she was staying in with her suitcase rolling behind her. She reached her room, slid the key into the lock, and opened the door.

"Hi Marilyn," Mike greeted from behind just as she stepped inside.

"Hi Mike and Brian," Cortney replied with a flirtatious smile. "Do you want to come in and smoke?"

"Sure," Mike agreed.

They entered the room, and the door closed behind them. A moment later, the door opened again just enough for Cortney to hang the "Do Not Disturb" sign on the doorknob before closing it firmly.

***

After getting done with her business at Walla Walla, Cortney headed for Seattle as planned. She exited the bustling terminal, her suitcase in tow when she saw Daryl waiting in his truck. He spotted her immediately and climbed out of the truck, his tall frame towering over the crowd. He took her suitcase and pulled her into a warm hug.

"Hey sis! How was your trip?" Daryl asked, his voice a mix of concern and curiosity.

"It's a trip. Literally and figuratively," Cortney responded with a hint of exhaustion but a smile on her face, nonetheless she was glad to be back and to see her brother again. Daryl and Cortney drove across the scenic water bridges into the city, with the sun shining down and the Seattle skyline coming into view. Kate Bush's "Running Up That Hill" played softly on the radio, setting a reflective mood as they headed toward Pike Place Market.

Later, they sat in a cozy fish restaurant, enjoying the ocean view from their table. The restaurant buzzed with the sounds of clinking glasses and murmured conversations.

"It's good to see you, sis," Daryl said, smiling warmly.

Cortney took a deep breath. "I'm thinking about moving here. I thought I would get a record deal with Playboy, but they want another model to sing my songs."

"If you want to launch a music career, this is the place to be. Are you still performing?" Daryl asked.

"I was, but my band got arrested for drug dealing," Cortney admitted with a sigh. "But I'm still singing telegrams, and I sing at a Chinese Taxi Dancing Club, too."

"Taxi Dancing?" Daryl raised an eyebrow.

"Yeah, it's part of Asian culture. They're nightclubs where girls can be hired by the minute plus tips. We dance and sing with the customers."

"Have you talked to Mom?" Daryl's expression turned serious.

"No," Cortney replied, her voice tense. "I got

sick a few years ago and asked her to care for me, and she said no. You know she would pimp me out as a kid? I'll never talk to her ever again."

"You know, she almost killed me when I was four." Daryl sighed heavily.

Cortney's eyes widened, a mixture of shock and sadness washing over her. The conversation hung heavily in the air, they both reflected on their troubled past, the sound of waves crashing gently in the background as the horrifying scene of almost getting killed by his mom flashed before his eyes.

In the dim light of an apartment in Prince George's County, a knock echoed through the small living room. Judi, 24, overweight but not pregnant, moved to open the door. Standing there were a lesbian couple, with little Daryl, just four years old, standing between them.

"Here is your adorable boy," said the first woman with a warm smile.

"Daryl was really good through the matinee." The second woman added.

"He ate black licorice and got it on his shirt," the first woman mentioned, pointing at the small dark stains on Daryl's shirt.

"Okay. Thank you. Bye," Judi replied curtly, closing the door quickly as the couple left. Her demeanor changed instantly. Fury radiated from her as she turned to face Daryl, who had already moved to sit on the worn sofa.

"Did you say 'thank you'?" Judi demanded, her voice tense and accusing.

Daryl looked down, his small hands fiddling with the hem of his shirt. "No," he mumbled.

Without warning, Judi grabbed a pillow off the sofa. Her eyes filled with rage, and she moved toward Daryl, pressing the pillow against his face. Daryl struggled beneath her weight, his tiny hands clawing at the pillow in a desperate attempt to breathe. The room seemed to close in, the walls silent witnesses to the horrifying act. Time stretched endlessly in those few moments of struggle, until finally, Judi released the pillow. Daryl gasped for air, tears streaming down his cheeks, the black licorice stain now an ironic reminder of the innocence he had lost.

Suddenly, Cortney shook Daryl's hand that brought him back to the present, as she sensed that her brother was zoning out. The large windows offered a stunning view of the ocean, the sunlight dancing on the waves. They picked at their plates, the crispy golden batter crunching with each bite.

"You know what Dad always says," Cortney began, her eyes meeting Daryl's across the table.

In perfect unison, they both recited, "What doesn't kill you makes you stronger," sharing a small, knowing smile.

Their conversation flowed easily, the setting sun casting a golden glow over their table. Despite the challenges and painful memories, they found solace in each other's company, drawing strength from their shared history and the simple yet profound wisdom their father had instilled in them.

After having food by the ocean, Cortney and Daryl arrived at Kurt Fenstad's house, the quaint exterior giving way to a cozy, lived-in interior. A knock at the door echoed through the room, and Kurt Fenstad quickly answered, welcoming them inside with a warm smile.

"It's so good to see you," Kurt Fenstad said, enveloping Cortney in a big hug. "You look great. Can I interest you in some mushroom tea?"

"Yeah, Kurt has bags of magic mushrooms," Daryl added, grinning.

"Really?" Cortney asked with intrigue.

"Magic mushrooms grow wild here," Daryl explained. "You want to pick the ones with the purple ring around the base of the head."

Kurt Fenstad nodded enthusiastically. "I trip every weekend, and each trip is different. Day tripping is the best. Let's do it."

"Let's do it," Cortney agreed, her excitement evident.

THE GATES OF NIRVANA'S PIT

"Let's do it," Daryl added.

As Cortney's song "Marvel Sky" played softly in the background, Kurt brought three coffee cups on a tray to the coffee table. They all sat down on the couch, the room filled with a sense of anticipation and camaraderie. They clinked their cups together in a cheerful toast and chugged the mushroom tea.

Moments later, the room began to transform. The walls seemed to ripple and breathe, and lights emanated from the TV, casting mesmerizing patterns on the ceiling. Laughter bubbled up from all three of them, filling the room with joyous sound. The psychedelic experience was taking hold, each moment bringing new waves of visual and emotional intensity. Suddenly, Cortney felt a wave of nausea. She jumped up and ran into the bathroom, shutting the door behind her. Kurt Fenstad and Daryl heard the unmistakable sounds of her throwing up, their laughter subsiding into concerned chuckles.

Kurt Fenstad looked at Daryl with a knowing smile. "First time jitters," he said softly, nodding towards the bathroom door.

After having an eventful trip it was finally time to go back and Cortney was headed for the airport. As the car pulled up to the terminal at Seattle International Airport, Daryl, Kurt Fenstad, and Cortney stepped out, their faces etched with a mix of farewell and anticipation. Kurt Fenstad and Daryl enveloped Cortney in warm hugs, wishing her well on her journey. With her suitcase in hand, Cortney bid them goodbye and made her way inside the terminal.

Hours later, the scene shifted to Los Angeles International Airport. Cortney emerged from the terminal and hailed a cab, her expression a mix of weariness and determination as she embarked on the next leg of her journey.

Back at Cortney's Century City apartment, a sense of homecoming filled the air as she opened the door. She was greeted by the joyful barks of her puppy and the playful antics of her kitten. With a sense of gratitude, she crossed the hall to her neighbor's door and knocked.

"Thank you for watching Gioia and Osiris for me," Cortney expressed her appreciation.

"You're welcome," her neighbor replied warmly. "I hope you had a good trip."

Cortney nodded, her mind already set on her next move. "Yes, so much so that I'm giving you my 30 days' notice."

Her neighbor looked surprised. "Are you sure you want to move?"

"Seattle is where the music scene is," Cortney explained, her voice tinged with excitement. "I feel it is a good career move if I want to be a famous singer."

Her neighbor's expression shifted, concern creeping in as he cautioned, "But Seattle has a serial killer on the loose!"

Chapter 3
Zoom Zoom

Beneath the surface lies a web of secrets,
waiting to be found

Cortney Page's song "Zoom Zoom" blared from the speakers in the busy Boeing parking lot, setting an upbeat tone for the day. Kurt Fenstad left work with his co-worker, Dave Anderson. They exchanged a few words before getting into their cars and Dave followed Kurt as they made their way to a dive bar.

The duo pull into the parking lot of a Renton bar, which is full of trucks and beat-up sedans. They search for a spot, eventually finding one at the far end. Stepping out of their cars, they exchanged a glance, knowing this bar is where they often unwind after a long day at Boeing. They headed toward the entrance, ready to escape the pressures of work for a while.

As Kurt and Dave stepped inside the dark and seedy bar, they saw that the place was packed with blue-collar workers. Kurt and Dave settled onto their bar stools and just then they exchanged nods with Gary Ridgway, a familiar face in the dimly lit surroundings. The air is filled with the smell of stale beer and cigarette smoke, mingling with the low hum of conversation. Just as they begin to relax into their seats, the door swings open, allowing a sliver of blinding sunlight to pierce the dim interior. Two prostitutes step inside, their forms outlined by the harsh light. They appeared as thin girls with shoulder-length hair tied in Madonna-like headbands who captivated everyone's attention.

The bartender, a burly man with a gruff demeanor leaned in as he asked, "What are you guys drinking today?"

"Coors Light for me," Kurt Fenstad responded with a casual shrug.

"I'll have the same, and I'll pay the ladies' tabs," Dave added, his eyes lingering on the girls.

"You mean those ladies of the evening?" he clarified.

Dave simply nodded in response, his gaze fixed on the bartender with a determined look.

Without further ado, the bartender served Kurt Fenstad and Dave their drinks, his movements efficient as he carried out their orders. With their drinks in hand, he then made his way over to the two women, pointing discreetly to Dave before retreating back behind the bar.

Meanwhile, Daisy and Alma, the two women, sauntered over to Dave, confidently exuding both allure and professionalism.

"Hi, I'm Dave Anderson," Dave introduced

himself with a friendly smile, extending his hand in greeting.

"I'm Daisy, and this is Alma," Daisy replied, her voice smooth and sultry as she returned Dave's handshake with a firm grip.

"This is my co-worker, Kurt Fenstad. We work nights at Boeing, and we just got off work," Dave explained, introducing Kurt with a casual wave of his hand.

"Nice to meet you, Kirk," Daisy said.

"It's Kurt the flirt, not Kirk the irk," Kurt interjected mischievously as he leaned back against the bar.

Dave wasted no time in getting down to business, as he broached the topic of payment. "What are your rates?" he inquired.

"One condom is $30, or two for $50," Daisy replied.

"Can my buddy use the second condom?" Dave asked, seeking clarification.

"Sure, I don't see why not," Daisy replied nonchalantly, her gaze flickering briefly towards Kurt before returning to Dave.

They all quickly finished their beers. Daisy leaves her friend behind and hoped into the front seat as Kurt courteously opened and shut the door for her.

Dave then pulled out of the parking lot and started driving down the road.

Soon after they made their way to Dave's apartment to do the deed. Dave unlocked his door and stepped into his one-bedroom apartment where the bright midday sunlight filtered through the windows. Daisy, following behind, couldn't help but notice the presence of cats in the apartment.

"You have cats."

"Is that a question or a statement?" Kurt responded with sarcasm.

"I have two cats. Why? Are you allergic?" Dave confirmed.

Daisy dismissed any concerns about allergies and remarked, "No, it just stinks."

"Are you sure that's not your pussy?" Kurt replied.

Daisy rolled her eyes, unamused, and redirected the conversation, "Who wants to go first?"

"Dave will go first. He's paying." Kurt decided.

Dave and Daisy headed to the bedroom, leaving Kurt alone in the living room where he switched on the TV, selecting a pornographic video, and began to entertain himself while waiting for his turn.

Suddenly, a loud thump resonated from the bedroom wall, startling Kurt. He jumped up in alarm, and the bedroom door swung open. Daisy emerged from the bedroom, completely naked, clutching her clothes.

"What the fuck was that?" Kurt asked with shock and concern evident in his voice.

"That was your friend killing his fucking cat," Daisy responded bluntly and left the house.

Kurt's expression morphed into a mixture of disbelief as Daisy's words sank in with confusion lingering in the air.

Meanwhile back at the Renton bar, Alma, the other prostitute, stood on the corner outside.

"Why does she have to leave me alone?" Alma muttered in annoyance while hailing a taxi. She got into it, but little did she know, it would be her last ride. The cab drove away, carrying her to her death.

**

At the Starlight Nightclub, Manny, the valet, efficiently took cars and issued tickets to the stream of arrivals. The scene was filled with an air of sophistication, with women resembling models and men predominantly of Asian descent. Jenna arrived in a sleek Jeep alongside Tonya, both dressed impeccably for the occasion. As they pulled up, Manny promptly opened Tonya's door.

"Is Cortney here? She's supposed to be back from Seattle," Tonya inquired with a hint of anticipation in her voice, eager to catch up with her friend.

"She has a singing telegram and will be coming later," Manny responded courteously, conveying the information.

"Oh, okay. I was just wondering. I always enjoy her songs," Tonya acknowledged, her overzealous fondness for Cortney's performances evident in her tone.

"What?" Jenna interjected, seeking clarification on the conversation.

"Manny was just saying that Cortney has a gig and is singing tonight, but she'll be late," Tonya explained to Jenna, ensuring everyone is on the same page.

"Better late than never," Jenna remarked with a smile.

"You, ladies, have a wonderful night," Manny bids them farewell as they head into the club.

Meanwhile, a navy blue Corniche Rolls Royce glided into the driveway, drawing attention with its elegance. David Shaw emerged from the vehicle, handed the keys over to Manny, and made his way toward the entrance of the building.

In the dimly lit interior of the Starlight

Nightclub, David Shaw caught the attention of the madam and signaled her.

"Is Cortney here tonight?" he inquired with anticipation.

"No, but Jenna and Tonya are here," she informed him with a smile. "If Cortney shows, she'll love you more for hiring her friends to join you. Make a welcome home party for her."

David's expression shifted slightly, "That Jenna is no friend to Cortney," he asserted firmly. "She wants what Cortney has, and that's a benefactor like me."

The madam's response was measured yet revealing, her words carrying an insight into the dynamics at play. "Everyone in the Philippines wants your sugar. Your family name is famous," she remarked casually.

"You've been to the Philippines?" he inquired, intrigued by her knowledge.

"No. Cortney told me," the madam clarified.

David's curiosity piqued, he realized the extent of Cortney's discussions about him. "So she does talk about me," he mused aloud, a note of satisfaction in his voice.

"Hell yeah! She gives me 10 percent of what you give her. I'm like her church," she quipped and they shared a laugh.

As they moved toward a secluded booth, the madam gestured for Jenna and Tonya to join them at David Shaw's table, signaling the beginning of an eventful evening at the Starlight Nightclub.

That evening, at the Starlight Nightclub, Cortney pulled into the driveway dressed as Marilyn Monroe. Manny, the valet, opened her door and handed her a ticket.

"David Shaw is here for the first time without his bodyguards," Manny informed her.

"I'm breaking things off with him tonight because I'm moving to Seattle," Cortney replied in a firm tone.

"Seattle? Where the Green River Killer lives?" Manny asked, raising an eyebrow.

"It's where the music scene is right now. If I want to be a famous singer, I must go where it can happen for me."

"L.A. is the entertainment capital. You don't need to go nowhere," Manny argued.

"Okay. The truth is I want to marry Bill Gates," Cortney admitted.

"The computer millionaire? That Bill Gates?" Manny asked, surprised.

"Yes, the same. I better get to work. I'm singing a song I wrote for him tonight," Cortney said, adjusting her dress.

"Who? David Shaw or Bill Gates?" Manny inquired, still puzzled.

"Both," Cortney replied with a mischievous smile.

"Whore," Manny whispered under his breath as she walked away.

I wasn't going to tell my friends, but I have been filming my torso dancing videos with music to reveal myself after six weeks of teasing my audience. I plan to air them on Seattle public access to entice the Green River Killer. I really am an adrenaline junkie. Why? Nevermind. She thought to herself while walking in.

Cortney, being an adrenaline junkie, always had a curiosity about the mysteries surrounding her. Her inquisitive nature often led her to many jackpots, but where there were positive aspects, there were negative ones too. And Cortney had not yet encountered any of those.

Inside the Starlight Nightclub, Cortney walked in, and the madam signaled her to follow her to David Shaw's table. Jenna and Tonya were drinking juice and smoking. Cortney approached David Shaw to kiss him on the cheek, but he turned his head, and they kissed on the lips instead, they held each other's gaze for a brief moment before the DJ's voice boomed through the club, "Cortney Page is going to sing her new song 'Happy Hearts' for us tonight. Hit it for Cortney."

As she sang, David Shaw's mind wandered to their sweet past together. He remembered them being on a plane, her laughter filling the air as he surprised her with a puppy, then the joy in her eyes when he bought her a kitten at the same pet shop. He recalled their shopping sprees on Rodeo Drive, her delight at every purchase, and the excitement of house hunting in Beverlywood, imagining a future together. Each memory was filled with happiness and warmth, showing their time together as a series of cherished moments.

When Cortney finished, the DJ announced, "Okay, folks, give it up for Cortney Page." Tonya was the only one clapping and smoking as Cortney returned to the table.

"I've got something to tell you all. I'm moving to Seattle," Cortney announced.

"Why didn't you just stay there?" David Shaw's expression turned sour as he asked, irritation clear in his voice.

"When did this decision come about?" Tonya looked surprised.

"Seattle has terrible weather and is full of fat people." Jenna frowned.

"I'm moving in with my cousin. I'll work as

a temp during the day and perform at night in local clubs until I get a record deal." Cortney explained.

"Okay, ladies, the party's over." David Shaw stood up, clearly displeased.

"I'm sorry, David. All good things come to an end," Cortney said softly.

"So is our evening. Goodbye. You all can leave now. Get out." David Shaw replied.

Cortney, Jenna, and Tonya made their way back to the waiting room area. David Shaw handed the madam some money, got up from the table, walked by the glass window of the waiting area as he ignored the girls and left the club.

Outside the Starlight Nightclub, Cortney, Jenna, and Tonya, ready to leave, handed their tickets to Manny, the valet, who went to fetch their Jeep.

"I really liked your song," Tonya said in a curious voice. "What is it called? 'Happy Hearts?'"

Cortney nodded, a small smile on her face.

"What's internet knowledge?" Jenna randomly asked, curious about the ongoing buzz around it.

"It's the future. It's like having the telephone directory or an atlas on your computer instead of paper ones. And someday we'll have a George Jetson's phone, too." Cortney explained.

"You are sure ahead of your time, girlfriend. But if you make more music like 'Happy Hearts,' I see a Grammy in your future." Tonya remarked, being impressed, while Jenna elbowed her lightly, signaling her to stop.

"Well, here's my car. Good night, Cortney. Drive safely," Jenna said as she and Tonya kissed Cortney on both cheeks before getting into their Jeep and driving away.

Manny returned from the back lot, looking concerned. "Cortney, I have some bad news. You've got a flat tire."

"Oh my god! It's two in the morning, and I don't want to deal with triple 'A' right now." Cortney groaned.

"I'll take you home." Manny offered.

"That would be great, but you can't stay the night," Cortney warned, half-joking.

"Then forget it. Get your own ride. Psyche! I'm just kidding. Of course, I'll get you home safe." Manny teased.

Parked inconspicuously around the corner was David Shaw's navy blue Corniche Rolls Royce. As Manny turned, the sleek vehicle's lights flickered on, illuminating the area. Without a sound, it began to trail behind Manny's car, silently following their route.

After a moderately long drive, Manny pulled into the driveway of Cortney's Century City apartment. She gave him a quick peck on the lips, then exited the car and headed inside. Manny drove away, leaving the scene. Moments later, David Shaw's car pulled up in front of the apartment building.

Inside her apartment, Cortney began to undress, removing her wig and eyelashes. She then turned on the water for a shower and stepped in, enveloped in the soothing warmth.

Unaware of the events unfolding outside, Cortney closed her eyes, letting the water flow over her tired body. Suddenly, a gunshot rang out, followed by a flash of light from the Rolls Royce parked just beyond her window.

Cortney remained in the shower, the sound of the water drowning out any echoes of the distant gunshot. Once she finished, she stepped out and made her way to bed, still nude. The events of the evening lingered in her thoughts, though she remained unaware of the disturbance outside.

***

The next morning in her Century City apartment, while doing her morning routine Cortney was interrupted by a knock at the front door. She quickly threw on a robe and made her way to the door, securing it with a chain before opening it slightly to see two men standing in the hallway, each holding FBI badges.

"Cortney Page?" one of the men queried.

"And you are?" Cortney responded cautiously.

"I'm Special Agent Callahan, and this is Special Agent Jackson," the man replied, urging her to open up.

Cortney complied, removing the chain and fully opening the door. "And what did I do to have the pleasure of your company, gentlemen?" she asked.

"A man was shot in the head last night in front of your apartment," Special Agent Callahan informed her.

"A David Shaw. Do you know a David Shaw?" Special Agent Jackson inquired.

Cortney pondered for a moment. "The name sounds familiar. I know a lot of David(s). Oh yeah. I think David Shaw is my neighbor."

"Did you get our calling card?" Special Agent Jackson asked.

"If you are talking about the search warrant, yes. I did. Listen, I don't do drugs or eat meat, for that matter," Cortney clarified.

"Have you ever shot a gun?" Special Agent Callahan questioned.

"Never. How is the man that got shot? This David Shaw," Cortney asked with concern, feigning ignorance on the fact that she was well aware of who David Shaw was.

"He's at the UCLA hospital in a coma," Special Agent Jackson responded.

"Are you sure you don't know him?" Special Agent Callahan pressed further.

"I know of him but don't know him," Cortney affirmed.

"Here's our card. If you remember anything else..." Special Agent Callahan handed her their card.

"I recommend you don't go anywhere and pray David Shaw survives," Special Agent Jackson advised.

"Will do, gentlemen," Cortney assured them as they departed.

Cortney maintained her composure in front of the officers, careful not to arouse any suspicion. However, as soon as they left, she closed the door and slid to the ground, her back pressed against it. Fear and worry gripped her as she contemplated what was to come, her thoughts consumed by concern for David Shaw's well-being. She remained cautious, knowing she couldn't afford to get involved with the police. Her plans for Seattle and her aspirations of becoming a big-shot celebrity were at stake, and she couldn't let anything derail them. As she sat on the floor, her mind raced with conflicting emotions, torn between her ambitions and the unsettling events unfolding around her.

Chapter 4
Knocking at the door of Nirvana

Every new encounter holds the promise of transforming dreams into reality

As Cortney's song "Flirting with Fire" played softly in the background, she, along with Jenna, Tonya, and Dina, meticulously packed boxes into a pod parked outside her Century City apartment. Amidst the hustle, laughter, and occasional sentimental moments, Cortney engaged in small talk with her friends, expressing her excitement for the journey ahead.

"I can't believe we're finally doing this," Cortney said as she sealed up another box.

"You're going to do amazing things in Seattle, girl. I just know it." Jenna nodded.

"Thanks, guys. I am going to miss you both." Cortney said as she hugged her friends tightly.

Shortly after, Manny arrived with Cortney's car, they loaded it with her belongings and her beloved pets. Cortney took a moment to say a heartfelt goodbye to her apartment, each step forward filling her with a mix of anticipation and nostalgia.

As she set off on her journey, the golden rays of the California sun fell on the road ahead. Cortney couldn't help but feel a surge of excitement coursing through her veins. Despite the sudden turn of events with David Shaw's shooting, she was determined not to let anything derail her dreams.

Driving through the beautiful farmlands of Central California, Cortney couldn't resist rolling down the windows of her convertible, allowing the warm breeze to tousle her hair. With her favorite songs on the radio, she cherished every moment of the drive, feeling the wind in her hair and the thrill of the open road.

As the miles passed by, Cortney's thoughts drifted to the future, where she envisioned herself standing in the spotlight, captivating audiences with her mesmerizing voice. With each passing mile, she felt one step closer to her ultimate goal of becoming a successful singer.

As the sun set and the stars twinkled above, Cortney continued her journey, fueled by her unwavering determination. Seeing the 'Welcome to Washington' sign up ahead, she couldn't contain her excitement for the new adventure waiting for her in the Evergreen State.

***

After a refreshing but tiring ride, Cortney finally arrived at Kurt Fenstad's two-bedroom apartment. She unlocked the door, lugging her pet crates inside. After tending to her pets' needs, she collapsed onto the sofa, exhausted from the day's events.

"Cortney? Wake up. Go to your room and sleep in your bed," Kurt Fenstad's voice jolted her awake.

"Okay," she mumbled, rubbing her eyes. "Did you just get home?" she asked sleepily.

"Yeah. It's my bedtime now. Good night," Kurt replied, heading towards his own room.

"You know what?" Cortney began, hesitating.

"What?" Kurt prompted.

"Never mind," she trailed off, already drifting back to sleep.

***

In the busy FBI office, Special Agent Jackson and Callahan made their way to their adjoining desks and just then a secretary approached them with a tip about the David Shaw shooting.

"We got a tip about the David Shaw shooting," she began.

"From Cortney Page?" Special Agent Jackson inquired.

The secretary shook her head. "No. From a Jenna or Jennifer King. She said that David Shaw was at the Starlight Nightclub the night he was shot."

"Starlight Club. Isn't that downtown?" Special Agent Callahan questioned.

The secretary confirmed, "Yes. It's a Chinese nightclub for taxi dancers."

"You mean a cover for prostitution," Special Agent Jackson remarked.

"We should check it out," Special Agent Callahan suggested.

"Here's the address. They open at 9 p.m. Jenna also said that Cortney was David Shaw's mistress, and she helped Cortney move to Seattle." The secretary said as she handed them the address.

"What? Do you have an address on her in Washington?" Special Agent Jackson's eyebrows rose in surprise.

"Not yet, but we are pulling phone records for both Cortney Page and David Shaw," the secretary replied.

"Thanks, Barbara," Special Agent Callahan said appreciatively.

"Just doing my job," Barbara replied with a smile.

As the night fell, the Special Agents pulled into the driveway of the Starlight Nightclub, where Manny promptly greeted them and handed Special Agent Jackson a ticket. As Manny parked their car, the agents made their way to the front door and entered.

Inside the nightclub, Jenna and Tonya sat in the waiting area, while the madam attended to a customer. Spotting the two white men at the front desk, she whispered under her breath, "Oh, shit. Cops," and approached them cautiously.

"Hello, gentlemen," she greeted, her voice barely above a whisper.

"Does a Cortney Page work here?" Special Agent Jackson inquired.

"I don't think so," the madam responded. "The girls don't usually use their real names, so I don't know."

"You must have W-9s on them, so can you please check? Thank you. We'll wait," Special Agent Callahan requested.

The madam retrieved a large plastic file and began sifting through the numerous forms, as she searched for any trace of Cortney Page among them.

Meanwhile, at Kurt Fenstad's apartment, Cortney Page sat alone at the dining table, picking at her dinner while flipping through the Yellow Pages, her finger circling various temporary agencies. The ringing of the phone interrupted her solitary meal, and she reached for the portable device.

"Hello?" Cortney answered, sounding tired.

"Hey, sis. How's it going?" Daryl's voice came through the receiver.

"Not good," Cortney replied, "My sugar daddy was shot in front of my LA apartment and is lying in a hospital in a coma."

"How did you find out?" Daryl inquired with curiosity.

"Two FBI agents showed up at my door," Cortney explained with frustration. "And, the same ones who messed up my place with their search warrant."

"What did you tell them?" Daryl asked, in a cautious tone.

"I told them I know of David Shaw but don't know him," Cortney confessed in a guilty voice. "I said I think he is my neighbor."

"So you lied to them," Daryl said with disappointment.

"Yes," Cortney admitted, her tone resigned. "And they told me not to leave the State, too."

Back at the Starlight Nightclub, the madam meticulously sifted through stacks of paperwork.

"I don't have a Cortney Page in my records. What is her legal name?" She inquired a furrow on her brow.

"Her driver's license is Cortney Page,"

Special Agent Jackson stated.

"Do you have any corporations?" Special Agent Callahan questioned.

"Let me check again," the madam replied as deftly flipped through the documents.

In another part of the city, Daryl lounged on the couch in his apartment, holding his portable phone.

"You know, if David dies, you look guilty as hell," Daryl remarked with concern.

"I didn't do it, and I didn't hear anything. I have no idea who shot David Shaw. Anyway, I believe the truth always prevails," Cortney responded, in a steady voice despite the turmoil in her mind.

Inside the Starlight Nightclub, the madam pulled out a form and handed it to the agents.

"Goddess Isis Inc.," Special Agent Callahan read aloud, studying the document.

"Goddess Isis. Isn't she black?" Special Agent Jackson asked in confusion.

"Not this one. I think we got our girl," Special Agent Callahan replied with a resolute expression.

"Can you make us a copy, please?" Special Agent Jackson requested, looking back at the madam.

THE GATES OF NIRVANA'S PIT

"Sure," the madam agreed, as she took the form back to make a copy.

Outside the Starlight Nightclub, the special agents exited the building after successfully gathering evidence and handed their ticket to Manny to fetch their car.

"Hey, do you know a David Shaw?" Special Agent Callahan asked.

"Yes. David Shaw is a regular customer here. He drives a different car every night, or so it seems," Manny replied.

"Were you working last Monday night? He's in a coma from a gunshot wound to the head," Special Agent Jackson said.

"Yes. It was the first time David Shaw came without bodyguards," Manny responded.

"Bodyguards? What does David Shaw do for a living?" Special Agent Jackson inquired.

"He is some big-shot lawyer," Manny explained.

"Criminal lawyer?" Special Agent Callahan probed.

"No. Personal injury attorney," Manny clarified.

"What about Cortney Page?" Special Agent Jackson asked.

"What about her?" Manny replied in a cautious tone.

"Did Cortney and David have a fight that night?" Special Agent Jackson continued to investigate.

"I wouldn't call it a fight. Cortney told everyone that she is moving to Seattle for her music career. She also told me that she wants to marry Bill Gates. David left early. He was really upset. I also had to drive Cortney home that night because she had a flat tire," Manny explained.

"Did you have a fight with David Shaw?" Special Agent Callahan asked with narrow eyes.

"Me? No. He doesn't even know my name," Manny said, shaking his head.

"What is your name?" Special Agent Jackson asked.

"Manny or Emmanuel Herrera," Manny replied.

"So, she was planning on moving before the shooting," Special Agent Callahan noted.

"No, sir. Cortney didn't shoot David Shaw. When he wakes up, he'll tell you the same thing. It wasn't Cortney that fired that gun," Manny asserted, his voice firm with conviction.

***

The next day, determined to find a job, Cortney walked into the Apple One Offices and approached the receptionist.

"Hi, I'm Cortney Page, and I'm here to see Shelia," she said.

"Ok, please have a seat," the receptionist replied. Picking up the phone, she added, "Cortney Page is here to see you."

"Hi, I'm Sheila." Sheila came out and shook Cortney's hand in a jiffy.

"Nice to meet you, Sheila," Cortney said.

"Follow me," Sheila instructed.

Cortney and Sheila walked to a small office. Cortney sat down, and Sheila left the room while Cortney took a test.

"Are you done?" Sheila asked as she returned after a short while.

"Yes," Cortney replied.

Sheila sat at her desk, while Cortney sat in a chair. "Looking at your scores, you did really well. Have we met before?" Sheila asked.

"Thank you, and I was famous in my past life," Cortney said, with a playful smile and they giggled together.

"What is your background work history?"

Sheila asked.

"I worked at recording studios and nightclubs. I worked for David Geffen -- we have the same birthday. I also worked at the Record Plant and called an ambulance for Axl Rose. Axl's doctor called and thanked me for saving his life," Cortney explained.

"Are you a musician?" Sheila inquired.

"Performing artist. I'm a Marilyn Monroe impersonator," Cortney replied.

"Yeah, now that you said that -- you look just like her. I have a long-term temp job available for you. It's at the Art Institute of Seattle as a receptionist," Sheila offered.

"I'll take it," Cortney agreed, her voice filled with determination.

***

Cortney pulled into the parking lot of the Art Institute of Seattle, observing the many students walking around. She stepped in and approached the front desk receptionist. "Hi, I'm Cortney Page and I'm your temp," she said.

"Great. I'm in accounting and just filling in for breaks and lunch. I'm Karla," the receptionist replied.

"Nice to meet you," Cortney said.

"You get an hour lunch, and you can smoke

at your desk. I'll cover you for restroom breaks, too. The agency said you know our phones," Karla explained.

Cortney nodded, sat down, and put on her headset.

Later that day, Cortney was eating her lunch in the kitchen when the music teacher, who was eating his sandwich, sat nearby.

"Hi, I'm Cortney Page," Cortney introduced herself.

"That sounds like a stage name," the teacher remarked.

"It's my name, and yes, I want to be on stage as a singer," Cortney replied.

"Do you have a demo tape?" the teacher asked.

"I sure do. Here, I've got one in my backpack," Cortney excitedly said, reaching into her bag.

"I'll listen to it after lunch and tell you what I think," the teacher promised.

With the lunch break now finished, Cortney was at the front desk taking calls when the teacher approached her.

"I like your music. It's original," the teacher said.

"Can you suggest any label that would sign me?" Cortney asked in a hopeful tone.

"Yes," the teacher replied. "I can set you up to meet with a new label called Sub Pop Records. They are down the street and within walking distance from here."

"Thank you so much. I really appreciate you doing this for me," Cortney said gratefully.

After doing most of her work for the day she used one of her breaks to visit Sub Pop Records. Cortney walked down the street and into the building. As she stepped inside she saw that the building was undergoing remodeling. Plastic hung from the ceilings, and the cement floors were bare. A stairway led to the second floor, where the partners had offices.

"Hi, I'm Bruce Pavitt. I got your demo from the music director at the Art Institute of Seattle," he said as he approached Cortney.

"And?" Cortney asked, her anticipation evident.

"I like it. I think the whole Goddess Isis theme goes with another band we represent," the Bruce continued.

"Oh really? What is the name of that band?" Cortney curiously inquired.

"Nirvana," the Bruce replied. "I'd like you to

meet up with Kurt Cobain, the lead singer, and write together. He is punk and you are techno-pop. But maybe together you could create your own new sound."

"Ok, great. What's his number? I'll give him a call," Cortney said enthusiastically.

Bruce wrote Kurt Cobain's number on the back of a Sub Pop business card and handed it to Cortney.

Returning to the Art Institute, Cortney sat at her desk, back to being a receptionist. Given her excitement, she couldn't wait until she got off work and instantly picked up the phone to dial Kurt Cobain's number.

"Hi, this is Cortney Page, and Sub Pop gave me your number," Cortney said, her voice steady. "They suggested we write some songs together. I work downtown at the Art Institute of Seattle as a receptionist."

She paused, listening to Kurt Cobain and replied. "Ok. I'll meet you tomorrow at the Moore Theater at noon. See you then," Cortney finished, a smile of anticipation spreading across her face as she hung up the phone and leaned back in her chair. She couldn't help but think to herself, just a few days in Seattle and I'm already meeting a band member. The excitement bubbled inside her, she knew she was ready to make the most of any opportunity that came her way.

Chapter 5
All I Wanna Do is Make Love to You

*Love is an irresistible desire to be
irresistibly desired.
—Robert Frost*

The next day, Cortney walked out of the Moore Theater with Kurt Cobain. The sun was shining brightly as they made their way to Pike Place Market, chatting casually.

At Pike Place Market, they found a quaint Greek restaurant with blue and white awnings. The air was filled with the smell of fresh produce and seafood from nearby stalls, surrounded by the lively chatter of market-goers.

"You know, I've been to Greece," Cortney said, breaking the silence between them.

"Oh yeah, what was it like?" Kurt Cobain asked curiously.

"I went with a girlfriend, and we had everything paid for," Cortney explained. "We didn't have to pay for food or our hotel. The men there are very generous. But we did get our butts pinched a lot," she added with a laugh.

"Say something in Greek," Kurt prompted, leaning in closer.

"Efcharisto is 'Thank you,' and Parakalo is 'You're welcome,'" Cortney replied, smiling at his interest.

"What time do you have to get back?" Kurt asked, glancing at his watch.

"I'm supposed to be back in an hour," Cortney said, checking the time herself.

"Do you think we'll have time for a nooner?" Kurt asked with a mischievous grin.

"If we leave now, we should have enough time," Cortney replied with excitement.

They walked back to the Moore Theater, where Kurt was renting a room off the side of the stage. The anticipation between them was strong, and Cortney couldn't help but feel a surge of excitement for what was about to happen.

"All I Wanna Do is Make Love to You" by Heart played softly in the background as Kurt and Cortney undressed and made love in Kurt Cobain's bachelor pad.

"Your birthmark is sexy," Kurt remarked, tracing it gently with his fingers.

"Yeah, the mark of the beast," Cortney replied. "If you look closely, you'll see three question marks in it."

"So, you're the devil?" Kurt teased.

Cortney smiled. "Devil spelled backwards is lived. I once lived as Marilyn Monroe, and I am the second coming of her."

"So you are both the resurrection of Marilyn Monroe and the anti-Christ?"

"Well, I'm a witch because I worship the goddess, Isis. So in a way, I am the 'anti-Christ.' I think praying to a dead man on a cross is abhorrent." Cortney replied.

"You better go. You're going to be late for work." Kurt said as he glanced at the clock.

"Okay, I'll leave," Cortney said, as she started to dress. "I'll see you tomorrow?"

"Yes," Kurt nodded. "Bring your notebook next time, so we can write backwards together."

As Cortney continued to put on her clothes, Kurt added with a smile, "Your carpet matches the curtains."

"Yep, I bleach my pubic hair to match my hair." Cortney chuckled.

Each day, Cortney entered the Moore Theater, carrying her notebooks. She left with them daily, filled with new ideas and the lyrics she and Kurt Cobain worked on together.

***

One sunny day, Cortney walked into Nordstrom department store, heading straight for the return department to fill out an application. She approached the counter, smiling at the woman behind it.

"Hi, I'd like to fill out an application for a part-time job," Cortney said.

The woman handed her a form. "Here you go. Just fill this out and bring it back to me when you're done."

Cortney thanked her and moved to a nearby counter to complete the application. After filling it out, she got back in line, glancing around the store. A blond man dressed in all white, wearing tennis shorts and sneakers, stood at the counter. Cortney noticed his legs and began twirling her hair, a habit she had when she was nervous or curious. As she stood there, soon after she realized the man was none other than Bill Gates.

"I bought this for my mother and would like to return it," Bill Gates said to the cashier.

This was the moment Cortney had been anticipating for a while and when it finally arrived she didn't lose one moment thinking about not trying her luck. Gathering her courage, Cortney walked up to him and tapped him on the shoulder. "Hi, I couldn't help but notice what a good son you are for buying

THE GATES OF NIRVANA'S PIT

your mother gifts instead of your girlfriend," she said with a friendly smile.

Bill turned to her, slightly surprised. "No, there is no girlfriend. I'm Bill, and you are?"

"Cortney Page. No 'U' or 'I' in Cortney Page," she replied.

"Nice to meet you, Miss Page," Bill said, shaking her hand.

"More like the missing page or the missing link," Cortney giggled.

Bill laughed softly. "Do you have time to take a train ride with me?"

"Sure. I'd love to." Cortney replied as her eyes widened in surprise and excitement.

Bill turned back to the cashier. "Thanks for the credit," he said, finalizing his return.

As they walked through the department store towards the train station, Cortney couldn't believe her luck. Here she was, in Seattle for just a short while, and already making connections she'd only dreamed of. The possibilities seemed endless and this unexpected encounter left Cortney buzzing with excitement.

Bill and Cortney got on the train together, blending into the bustling crowd, luckily they found seats next to each other. The steady clatter of the train set a backdrop to their conversation.

"What do you do, Cortney?" Bill asked as they settled into their seats.

"I'm a temp to pay the bills, but I'm an aspiring singer and actress from Los Angeles," Cortney replied, her voice full of determination.

"Are you single?" Bill inquired, curiosity evident in his tone.

"No. I have a boyfriend."

"And what does he do?" Bill continued, leaning slightly closer.

"He's a musician," Cortney said.

"But how does he pay his bills?" Bill asked.

"He's a nighttime janitor for office buildings," Cortney explained.

Bill looked thoughtful for a moment before saying, "I'd really like to take you to dinner."

"That would be nice. I'd like that, Bill," Cortney replied as her eyes lit up.

Bill handed Cortney his business card but she offered him her number instead, "Take my cellular number?" she said.

"You have a cellular phone?" Bill asked in surprise.

"Yes, my boyfriend gave it to me," Cortney answered with a smile.

The train rumbled on, carrying them through the city as they exchanged more details about their lives. Cortney felt a rush of anticipation building inside her, she had a feeling that this encounter was the beginning of something significant.

***

The next day's sun was out, shining brightly, and so was Cortney, radiant in her Chanel attire. With a determined stride, she made her way to the radio station, the anticipation of what the day might hold adding an extra spring to her step. As she stepped into the busy radio station, she approached the reception desk where a friendly face greeted her.

"Hi, I'm your temp, Cortney Page," she introduced herself with a warm smile.

The receptionist nodded in acknowledgment. "Hi, you'll be doing data entry. It is down the hall, first door on your left," she directed Cortney.

Following the directions, Cortney made her way down the hall, her heels clicking against the floor. Just as she entered the office, another figure entered behind her.

"Hi, I'm Bob and I'm the program manager," the man introduced himself.

"Hi Bob, I'm Cortney Page, also known as

Goddess Isis," Cortney turned to greet him.

"So, you're an artist?" he inquired.

"Singer and songwriter. I'm a performing artist; more like spoken word with a goddess message. Here's my demo, and here's my boyfriend's music." Cortney replied with confidence.

Bob's curiosity piqued as Cortney handed him the materials. "Nirvana. Huh? I'll give them a listen. You never know," he remarked, his interest sparked by the unexpected encounter.

Cortney's days in Seattle were becoming more intertwined with her growing connection to Bill Gates. Their conversations had taken a flirty turn, and their upcoming dinner date was a promising step forward in their budding romance. Each phone call between them felt like a prelude to something deeper, something more significant.

At his office, Bill picked up the phone and dialed a number, his office filled with the soft hum of computers and the distant chatter of employees.

"Hi, it's Bill," he said, leaning back in his chair.

Meanwhile at the Radio station, Cortney was on her cellphone, seated at her desk amidst the buzzing activity of the radio station.

"Hi, Bill. I was just thinking about you. I'm glad you called," she replied while twirling her hair.

"I want to take you to dinner Friday night," Bill said.

"I would love to, but I'm performing at a club for Entertainment Television," Cortney explained, a little regretful in her tone.

"How about Saturday?" Bill suggested.

"Ok. It's a date. I'll see you Saturday. What's your address?" Cortney asked, grabbing a pen and paper. She wrote down the address Bill provided and hung up just as Bob entered the room.

"I really like the Nirvana tape you gave me and will put it on the station playlist," Bob said in an enthusiastic tone as he approached her desk.

"What about my music?" Cortney asked, hopeful.

"Sorry, Cortney, but you just don't have musical talent," Bob replied bluntly, his words cutting through the air.

Cortney felt a sting of disappointment but maintained her composure, nodding as Bob walked away. The buzzing of the radio station continued around her, a stark contrast to the quiet determination she felt inside.

***

It was finally Friday night, the time for Cortney's first ever performance in Seattle. A TV truck was parked out front, and a crowd lined up to get in, creating a buzz of anticipation. Daryl and Kurt Fenstad drove Cortney into the parking lot. The neon lights of the Seattle Waterfront Nightclub glowed brightly in the night, casting colorful reflections on the wet pavement. As they approached the entrance, the murmur of excitement from the crowd filled the air.

They went straight to the front of the line, where a bouncer stood guard. Cortney stepped forward with a confident smile.

"Hi, I'm singing today," she said, her voice clear and assertive.

The bouncer looked her over and nodded. "You want to talk to the press first?" he asked.

"Sure," Cortney agreed, glancing towards the news truck nearby.

The bouncer pointed to the reporter, who was already broadcasting from beside the truck. Daryl and Kurt Fenstad headed into the club while Cortney walked over to the truck, her heart pounding with excitement.

"Hi, I'm singing tonight," Cortney said as she approached the news crew.

The anchorwoman turned to her with a smile. "Great. What's your name, Marilyn?" she asked in a teasing tone.

"I'm Cortney Page, but my stage name is Goddess Isis," Cortney replied and the lights went on, spotlighting her and the reporter, and the camera started to film.

"We are here at Seattle's Waterfront Nightclub with Goddess Ice," the reporter announced.

"Goddess Isis," Cortney corrected gently.

"Tell us about yourself," the anchorwoman prompted.

"I believe I'm the reincarnation of Marilyn Monroe, and, according to mythology, Goddess Isis is the first reincarnation story," Cortney explained.

"You look just like her," the reporter observed.

"I've got the same birthmarks in the mirror, too," Cortney added with a confident smile.

"What will you be singing tonight?" the anchorwoman asked.

"I'm singing 'The Most,' which is about dating more than one man," Cortney revealed with a mischievous grin.

"Is that true about you?" the anchorwoman asked.

"Not yet, but it's about to be," Cortney said with a giggle, her infectious laughter drawing smiles from the news crew.

As the interview wrapped up, the reporter thanked her and she made her way into the club, feeling a rush of exhilaration. The night was young, and Cortney knew it was just the beginning.

The interior was glowing with vibrant neon lights. Cortney, Daryl, and Kurt Fenstad made their way to the bar and ordered drinks, the room steadily filling with people. The atmosphere buzzed with energy as patrons chatted and laughed, the anticipation of the night's performances was evident in the vibe inside.

The MC took the stage, his voice echoing through the speakers. "Hello everyone. Thank you for coming tonight. Our first act is a goddess from Los Angeles. Please give a warm welcome to Goddess Isis."

Cortney walked up on stage, the spotlight illuminating her as the music began to play. She took a deep breath and started to sing.

"…Sitting on my sofa, drinking tall mimosas, I'm a joke at times, pretending my lines, la la la, la la la, I love you the most, I love you the most, sewing wild oats, I love you the most…"

"Boo. Boo. Whore." A grunge guy heckled loudly from the back of the room.

Cortney continued, her voice unwavering.

"…I love you, I love you, I love you…"

Daryl noticed the commotion and went over to the grunge guy, with a stern face. "That's my sister singing," He said.

"She sucks, and her song sucks," The grunge guy sneered.

Without a second thought, Daryl threw a punch, connecting with the grunge guy's jaw, shattering his ego in one shot. The scene went black as chaos erupted in the club.

***

The next day, Daryl sat in the holding cell at Kings County Jail, the cold metal bench beneath him a reminder of the previous night's chaos. A small TV mounted high on the wall played the news.

There are sixteen missing girls and twenty eight skeletons found. They are all found connected to the Green River Killer.

Daryl's attention was drawn away as the cell door creaked open.

"You've been bailed out," a deputy announced, standing at the threshold.

As Daryl walked out of the jail, the midday sun casting long shadows on the ground, he spotted Cortney and Kurt Fenstad standing by Cortney's car. Relief washed over him, and they embraced tightly.

"Let's get out of here," Cortney said with concern.

They hopped into the car, and Cortney started the engine. As they drove away, the cold, gray building of the jail quickly receded into the distance.

***

Cortney drove up to the gate of Bill Gates' home on the lake and pressed the intercom button. The house was nestled among towering pine trees, with a winding driveway leading up to it. The soft glow of the street lights reflected on the water, creating a picturesque scene. The gentle lapping of the lake against the shore added to the tranquility, while the grand facade of the house, illuminated by lights, exuded elegance and opulence.

"Hello," Bill Gates' voice crackled through the intercom.

"I'm here with my dog," Cortney replied.

The gate opened, and Bill came out from around the corner with two Doberman pinschers by his side. He walked over to Cortney's car, the dogs trotting obediently beside him.

"I'm scared of big dogs," Cortney admitted as Bill approached.

"They won't hurt you," Bill assured her. He opened the car door, and she stepped out, hugging him tightly. He kissed her gently, and she felt a sense of security despite the imposing dogs.

After leaving Bill Gates' home on the lake, Bill and Cortney walked up to the hostess stand at a high-end Seattle restaurant. The restaurant's interior was elegant, with dim lighting that gave a warm glow to the sophisticated decor.

"Hi, we have reservations for two," Bill said to the hostess.

"This way, please," the hostess responded, leading them to a table with a stunning view of the waterfront. The lights from the boats and buildings reflected off the water, adding to the evening's charm.

Bill pulled out a chair for Cortney, and she sat down as the hostess handed them menus.

"You look lovely tonight," Bill remarked with admiration.

"Thank you. I don't have much to wear. Everything is in storage," Cortney said.

"I'd like to give you a credit card to do some shopping," Bill offered generously.

"That is a very generous offer," Cortney replied, touched by his kindness. She glanced at the menu and noticed the absence of prices. "There are no prices on the menu."

"Don't worry about the cost. Order whatever you want," Bill reassured her.

"I don't eat meat, but I do eat fish because they don't have feelings. I'll have the soup and salad. I'll let you order for me," Cortney said, handing the decision over to Bill.

He smiled and nodded, appreciating her trust. As the waiter approached, Bill began to place their order, and Cortney felt a sense of anticipation for the evening ahead.

Bill Gates' home on the lake was a modern architectural masterpiece, surrounded by tall pine trees with panoramic water views. As Bill and Cortney pulled into the driveway, moonlight reflected off the lake, creating an enchanting atmosphere. They got out of the car and walked towards the grand entrance.

"Come in for a nightcap," Bill suggested as they reached the door.

"Thank you, but I don't drink," Cortney replied with a polite smile.

"Well then, come in for a smoke," Bill offered, his eyes gleaming.

"OK," Cortney agreed.

Inside, the living room was a blend of luxury and cutting-edge technology. As they sat down, a hidden compartment in the furniture opened, revealing a sleek TV that rose from the floor. Cortney took out a cigarette, and Bill took the cigarette and lit it for her and gave it back. The room was filled with a soft, ambient light that added to the intimate setting.

They began kissing, but after a moment, Cortney pulled back, a mixture of emotions flickering in her eyes.

"I really like you. I want to take care of you," Bill said earnestly, his gaze steady on hers.

"I really like you, too, but I have a boyfriend," Cortney confessed in a soft and hesitant voice.

"You told me. But I can offer you so much more," Bill insisted, reaching into his pocket. He took out his wallet and handed her a credit card.

"Here is my credit card. You can use it," Bill said, in a gentle but persuasive tone.

Cortney looked at the card in her hand, a sense of amazement and gratitude washing over her. "Thank you so much. You really do like me," she said.

Bill smiled, pleased with her reaction. "I do," he affirmed, leaning back on the sofa. The moment was charged with unspoken possibilities, the lake outside a silent witness to the unfolding drama.

Chapter 6
Cortney and Courtney

Life is a journey that must be traveled
-Oliver Goldsmith

The next day, Cortney sat at a makeup counter in Nordstrom, her reflection framed by a halo of bright lights. A skilled salesperson applied the finishing touches to her look. Cortney admired the transformation in the mirror, her eyes sparkled with satisfaction.

"I'll take it all," Cortney declared, a smile spreading across her face.

Her next stop was the salon, where the stylist carefully colored her hair. The hum of hair dryers and the scent of shampoo filled the air. After her hair was washed and blow-dried, she left the salon with shopping bags in hand, heading straight for the jewelry counter.

"Do you have gold cufflinks?" Cortney asked the salesperson.

Later that day, Cortney found herself in a thrift store, rifling through racks of clothing. She selected a dozen flannel shirts, a whimsical contrast to her earlier luxury shopping spree. With two trash bags full of her purchases, she left the store.

Cortney then drove through the city, the shopping bags strewn across the backseat, just then her cell phone rang breaking the silence.

"Hello," she answered, balancing the phone against her ear.

"Hey, how's it going?" Kurt Cobain's voice came through the speaker.

"Good. I'm shopping, and I've bought you a few things," Cortney replied, her voice filled with affection.

"I've been thinking that we should break up. Since you changed jobs, we never see each other anymore," Kurt Cobain said abruptly.

Cortney's heart skipped a beat, a wave of shock washing over her. "You break up with me, Kurt, and then call like nothing's happened. I must tell you something," she said.

"What?" Kurt Cobain said.

"Never mind," Cortney replied, the words catching in her throat and she ended the call.

Kurt Cobain, sitting in the cluttered living room of his bachelor pad, hung up his portable phone and, in a fit of frustration, threw it across the room. The device skidded to a halt against the far wall, amid scattered clothes and musical equipment.

***

THE GATES OF NIRVANA'S PIT

Cortney sat at the small kitchen table of Kurt Fenstad's cluttered apartment, flipping through a stack of music magazines. The lamp nearby gave the room a dull yellow glow, accentuating the coziness of the space. She circled an ad for an audition with a red pen and then picked up the phone, dialing the number listed.

"Hi, I'm calling about the ad for the audition," Cortney said in a steady but hopeful voice.

"Yeah? Who do you sound like?" a woman asked on the other end.

"I've been told my songs are similar to Stevie Nicks," Cortney replied confidently.

"What's your name and story?" the woman inquired.

"I'm Cortney Page, and I'm from L.A. I look like Marilyn Monroe. Rockwell, or Kennedy Gordy, Barry Gordy's son from Motown, was my manager until the rest of my band got arrested for selling drugs," Cortney explained.

"I'm Courtney Love. Ok. I'll give you a chance. Go see Frank at Seattle Central College tomorrow night," the woman responded.

Cortney's heart raced with a mix of excitement and nerves. "Thank you, Courtney." She said before hanging up the phone. She leaned back, a confident smile lighting up her face as she looked at the circled ad, imagining the possibilities ahead.

***

The following night, Cortney stood nervously at the piano in the dimly lit practice room of Seattle Central College, her fingers hovering over the keys, when Frank walked in.

"Hi, I'm Frank," he greeted, eyeing Cortney with a curious expression.

"Cortney Page. Nice to meet you." Cortney replied.

Frank struck a piano key, prompting Cortney to sing.

"Do, Re, Mi, Fa, So, La, Ti," she sang softly as her voice resonated through the room.

After Cortney left, Frank sat in his office and dialed a number on his phone.

"Hi, Courtney, I auditioned Cortney Page, and she can't sing. You sound better than her. You should be the bands lead singer."

***

After getting done with the audition, Cortney walked into Kurt Fenstad's apartment, greeted by her enthusiastic dog. She picked up the phone and dialed a number.

"Hi, it's me," Cortney said warmly, her voice

tinged with disappointment.

Courtney Love sat in her dad's house, the room was dimly lit and filled with a haze of cigarette smoke. The phone rang, breaking the silence. She picked it up and answered, "Hello?" in a casual tone.

"Hi, Courtney," Cortney said with uncertainty. "I didn't make it past the audition, but I wanted to invite you to see my boyfriend's band play. They're called Nirvana."

"Nirvana? I know the band." Courtney Love said in a curious tone.

Cortney continued, her voice determined. "I'll pick you up this Friday."

"I've got another party to attend that night," Courtney Love replied.

"We can do both. I won't take no for an answer," Cortney insisted.

"Okay, then," Courtney Love conceded in a resigned voice and lit a cigarette, pondering the invitation.

Cortney was back on the phone, jotting down directions on a notepad. The apartment was quiet, except for the occasional rustle of paper and the faint hum of the refrigerator.

***

The morning light filtered through the blinds,

bathing the bedroom in a soft glow where Gioia and Osiris, her pets, were curled up on the bed next to Cortney. The tranquility was interrupted by the ring of her cell phone.

"Hello," Cortney answered, her voice still groggy from sleep.

Bill Gates sat at his sleek, modern desk, a panoramic view of the city behind him. He smiled as he spoke into the phone.

"Good morning, sunshine," Bill Gates said cheerfully.

"Good morning. My dad used to say that every morning to wake me up," Cortney randomly said as she was reminded of her father.

"I won't say it anymore," Bill responded, slightly concerned.

"I didn't mean it like that," Cortney reassured him.

Cortney got out of bed still on the phone with Bill, careful not to disturb her sleeping pets, and made her way to the kitchen. Soon after both of them woke up and as she began feeding Gioia and Osiris, the landline phone rang.

"Bill, I love talking to you, but I've got to go," Cortney said, ending the call on her cell phone. She then picked up the landline. "Hello, this is Cortney speaking."

Kurt Cobain was pacing in his cluttered living room, his portable phone gripped tightly in his hand. His voice was tense and accusatory.

"Who the fuck are you on the phone with? You know I see the phone log, so just tell me," Kurt Cobain demanded.

"You know what?" Cortney said, her patience wearing thin.

"What?" Kurt responded in a sharp voice.

"Never mind," Cortney said, in a dismissive tone as she hung up the phone.

Later that night, Cortney pulled up in front of Courtney Love's dad's house and honked the horn. Her dog resting between her neck and the headrest. Courtney Love, 26, stepped out, dressed like Madonna, and hopped into the car as they drove away.

People walked into Officer Craig's house, where a party was in full swing. Inside his house, Courtney Love and Cortney Page made their way to the kitchen amidst departing guests, but Officer Craig remained.

"Hey Craig. How the hell are you?" Courtney Love greeted him.

"I'm good, and who's that, your twin sister?" Officer Craig asked.

"No, this is my friend, also a Cortney," Courtney Love explained.

"What can I do for you girls? Can I get you a drink?" Officer Craig offered.

"I don't drink," Cortney declined.

"I'll have a coke with a straw," Courtney Love requested. Officer Craig mysteriously handed a folded piece of paper to Courtney Love, who kissed him on the cheek.

"Thanks, Craig, we've got to go," Courtney Love said.

"Yeah, my boyfriend is playing at the Moore Theater," Cortney excitedly added.

Outside the Moore Theater, crowds of people gathered, forming a buzzing sea of anticipation. Cortney Page and Courtney Love had to walk several blocks from where they parked the car to reach the venue.

Inside the Moore Theater, Nirvana took the stage, greeted by the thunderous cheers of the crowd. Kurt Cobain's guitar strings reverberated through the air, signaling the start of the performance.

Amidst the cheering crowd, heckles of "Cortney, Cortney, Cortney…" and other taunts erupted sporadically, adding an unexpected twist to the atmosphere. Cortney Page and Courtney Love hurried through the audience towards the back of the stage, seeking refuge in the bathroom.

Inside the dimly lit bathroom, Cortney checked each stall for any eavesdroppers.

"What the fuck is that all about?" Courtney Love asked in equal amounts of confusion and surprise.

Cortney sighed, feeling the weight of her situation. "I have two boyfriends. They know about each other. Bill gave me his credit card and Kurt gave me my cell phone, so he sees the phone calls, so he knows."

"Bill who?" Courtney Love asked, her eyebrows furrowing in disbelief.

"Bill Gates. We haven't had sex yet, but I really want to. I'm a sugar baby that doesn't have sex for money. If he was my sugar daddy, then it means I'm a kept woman," Cortney explained in an uncertain voice.

***

Inside Kurt Cobain's bachelor pad, Kurt entered through the door, finding Cortney Page and Courtney Love smoking. Courtney Love rose to depart as she greeted Kurt.

"Kurt, this is Courtney, too," Cortney introduced.

Kurt nodded in acknowledgment. "Hi, how's

it going?" he greeted casually.

"Hi. I was just leaving," Courtney Love replied, making her way into the hallway.

"Let's rage," Courtney Love said, retrieving a folded paper from her bra before departing.

After Courtney Love left, Kurt closed the door and lit a joint, filling the room with the pungent smell of smoke. He looked at Cortney with frustration and suspicion and his brows furrowed. Grabbing a condom from his dresser, he pinned it with caution, his anger simmering as he realized Cortney had been in touch with Bill Gates.

"Get undressed. Get into bed," Kurt instructed Cortney in an authoritative tone.

Cortney and Kurt reclined on the bed together, their lips meeting in a passionate kiss as Kurt began to undress.

"Turn off the lights. I like it better in the dark. It's less dangerous," Cortney murmured.

***

The next morning, Cortney Page and Courtney Love exited the Moore Theater, the energy of the night still buzzing around them as they walked back to the car.

"Did you have fun?" Cortney asked, with a smile on her lips.

"Yeah, it was a blast. I've been up all night, just like everyone else, except for you and your boyfriend," Courtney Love replied.

Cortney nodded, a hint of contemplation in her eyes. "I do love him, but I have feelings for Bill, too."

"If you don't want Kurt, I'll gladly take him off your hands," Courtney Love teased.

Later, in Cortney's apartment, she was fast asleep, her furry companions curled up beside her when her phone rang.

"Hello?" she answered groggily.

"Hello, sweetheart. Do you want to have lunch and take a drive to my property?" Bill Gates' voice came through the phone. She responded with a mumbled yes before going back to sleep.

A little while later, at Bill Gates' lake house, Cortney drove in as the gate opened, and Bill emerged from the house. They both got into Bill's car, and as they drove away, the gates closed behind them.

At Bill Gates' property, Cortney and Bill strolled in the backyard when a neighbor approached.

"Hey, Bill," the neighbor greeted.

"Did you know your house is eight inches within my property line?" Bill Gates asked in a firm tone.

The neighbor shrugged. "What do you want me to do about it?"

"Move your house!" Bill Gates stated bluntly, his authority evident in his voice.

On their drive, Bill was behind the wheel, his expression focused as he navigated the road, while Cortney sat in the passenger seat with her dog in her arms.

"Are you really going to make your neighbor move his house?" Cortney asked out of curiosity.

"Yep, he needs to get off my property, even if it's only eight inches. I hope you like the house," Bill replied.

"I like your lake house better. Penny for your thoughts," Cortney said, her gaze fixed on him.

"Will you do something for me?" Bill asked, turning to look at her.

Cortney raised an eyebrow. "Like what?"

"I want you to spy on a competitive company for me," Bill revealed in a low and serious voice.

"I'll do it as long as no one gets hurt," Cortney agreed in a determined expression.

***

Cortney sat at a table in the Seattle Library, surrounded by books on religion, demonology, witchcraft, and baby names. She flipped through the pages, absorbing the information, before gathering the books and heading to the checkout desk.

As night fell, Cortney found herself in Bill Gates' Lake house, surrounded by a pile of books on both sides of the bed. Together, Cortney and Bill lay side by side, deeply engrossed in their respective reads.

"Let me teach you to speed read," Bill suggested, breaking the silence.

"Okay. But I'm reading baby names," Cortney responded, her attention still on the book in her hands.

"Oh, yeah? What baby names stand out to you?" Bill inquired with curiosity.

"I like Katherine the Great, Rory from 'Midnight Cowboy,' and Phoebe from the movie 'Lace.' You know what name I don't like?" Cortney replied, sharing her thoughts.

"What name is that?" Bill asked.

"Emma," Cortney stated firmly.

"I like Emily," Bill offered.

Cortney chuckled. "Yeah, you're right. Emily is a much better name."

As Cortney got off the bed and headed toward the bathroom, she remarked, "Got to pinch a loaf."

"Where did you hear that phrase?" Bill raised an eyebrow.

"Kurt," Cortney replied casually.

"Have you seen him?" Bill asked as he shifted.

"You know what?" Cortney asked.

"What"

"Never mind." With that, Cortney shut the bathroom door, leaving Bill alone with his thoughts.

***

In the dimly lit, smoky atmosphere of the Portland club, Kurt Cobain stepped off the stage, his face flushed with the adrenaline of the performance. The dim, smoky atmosphere of the club buzzed with post-concert energy. As he made his way through the crowd, Courtney Love approached him with a determined look and without warning, she punched him in the stomach.

Later that night, Kurt and Courtney sat around a rickety table in a room of the Portland motel. The air was thick with the smell of cigarettes and the acrid scent of speed. They were both lost in their highs, snorting lines and chain-smoking.

"I like you," Kurt said, his voice rough and

earnest. "I really, really like you"

Courtney looked at him, her eyes glassy but filled with a fierce intensity. "I like you, too," she replied. "You know, I'm in town to see my boyfriend play."

Kurt's eyes narrowed, though there was a playful glint in them. "I knew it," he said.

Courtney leaned closer, her breath warm against his face. "Who is my boyfriend?" She asked.

A slow mischievous smile spread across Kurt's face. "Me," he replied.

The tension between them broke as they lunged at each other, tearing at each other's clothes with a desperate urgency. Their hands roamed over each other's bodies, exploring with an intensity born of both passion and need. The flimsy motel bed creaked under their weight as they tumbled onto it, their movements frantic and uncoordinated at first.

Courtney's fingers dug into Kurt's back, leaving red marks in their wake, while he traced a line of kisses down her neck. Their breathing grew heavier, mingling with the sounds of the city outside the thin motel walls. Each touch, each kiss, each caress seemed to ignite a deeper hunger in them, driving them to the brink of madness.

In that moment, surrounded by the chaos of their lives and the squalor of the motel room, they found a fleeting connection, a raw and primal expression of their emotions. Their lovemaking was intense and passionate, a desperate attempt to hold on to something real in a world that often felt unreal. As they finally lay together, spent and breathless, the world outside seemed to fade away, leaving just the two of them in the quiet aftermath of their desire.

Chapter 7
Champaign and Confusion

*In the midst of chaos, there is also
opportunity*

-Sun Tzu

Courtney Love, Kurt Cobain, and a real estate
agent stood outside a charming house by the lake,
with a "For Sale" sign staked in the front yard. The
clear, calm waters of the lake glistened in the
background. They exchanged polite handshakes
before heading inside to inspect the property.

Inside, Courtney Love and Kurt Cobain were
busy holding hands and kissing each other. The
spacious living room offered a stunning view of the
lake, with large windows allowing natural light to
flood the space. The real estate agent cleared her
throat, drawing their attention.

"Look at this amazing view of the lake," the
agent said, gesturing towards the windows. "You
know, Bill Gates lives directly across the lake."

"The Great Gatsby," Kurt Cobain whispered,
his eyes fixed on the house across the lake.

Courtney Love smiled and turned to the agent.
"We'll take it," she said decisively.

As they left the house, Courtney Love and Kurt Cobain got into their car, their hands entwined. They pulled out of the driveway, leaving behind the real estate agent, who began taking down the "For Sale" sign. The lake house now belonged to them, a new chapter in their unconventional love story.

Meanwhile, outside Kurt Fenstad's apartment, Cortney was on her cell phone, her voice animated as she chatted. Beside her, Kurt Fenstad, sporting a Walkman, moved rhythmically to the music only he could hear. They crossed the parking lot, heading towards the community gym, waving at a friendly neighbor as they passed.

Inside the gym, Cortney continued her phone conversation, her voice echoing slightly in the open space. Kurt began his workout, his focus on the weights and machines.

"Where are you right now?" Bill Gates' voice crackled through the phone.

"At the gym," Cortney replied in a casual tone.

There was a pause on the other end before Bill spoke again. "Cortney Page, will you marry me?"

Cortney's eyes widened in surprise and delight. "Yes!" she yelled, her voice filled with excitement.

Kurt Fenstad, who was startled, removed his

headset and looked at her. "What?"

Cortney quickly turned away, her excitement now subdued. "Never mind," she said as her voice dropped to a whisper trying to process the sudden proposal.

The next day, Cortney stood at the receptionist's desk in Wang Office, juggling multiple calls with practiced ease.

"Thank you for calling Wang. Can you hold? Thank you for calling Wang. Can you hold? Thank you," she repeated, her tone professional and brisk. Suddenly, she noticed a call from Bill.

"Bill? Ok. I'm going to the bathroom," Cortney said into the phone, her voice dropping to a whisper. She quickly grabbed her Chanel pocketbook and headed towards the door.

As she stepped outside, four police cars screeched to a halt in front of the building, their lights flashing urgently. Eight officers jumped out and made their way into the building, their faces set with determination.

Cortney waited anxiously for the elevator, glancing around nervously. As the doors opened, she stepped inside just as the police officers emerged from another elevator down the hall and marched towards the Wang offices.

Cortney exited the building, her heart

pounding. She crossed the street quickly and got into her car, parked just across the way. With a quick glance back at the building, she started the engine and drove away, the tension in her shoulders slowly easing as she put distance between herself and the scene.

Later that night, Cortney and Bill sat in the living room of Bill Gates' lake house. Bill lit Cortney's cigarette and handed it to her.

"What was all that today?" Cortney asked, taking a drag.

"Precaution," Bill replied in a calm and reassuring tone.

"Did we do something that got me in trouble?" Cortney's brow furrowed with concern.

"No. You didn't get arrested, so everything is fine," Bill assured her.

"Promise me, you've got my back," Cortney said in a vulnerable tone.

"I've got your back, and you've got my heart," Bill responded with a soft smile.

"I love you. Penny for your thoughts," Cortney said, her tone softening.

"I think we should celebrate. I'll open a bottle of champagne," Bill suggested as he stood up in excitement.

"You know I don't drink," Cortney reminded him.

"You must join me. I insist," Bill said, his eyes twinkling as he popped the cork and began to pour three glasses.

Just then, there was a knock at the door. Bill opened it, and Warren Buffet walked in.

"Just in time," Bill said, a smile spreading across his face. "Warren, this is my fiancée, Cortney. Cortney, this is my closest friend, Warren Buffet."

"Nice to meet you," Cortney said, offering a polite smile.

She chugged the champagne and quickly became intoxicated. As she started to feel dizzy, a priest entered the living room. The room began to spin around her, and she struggled to focus on what the priest was saying.

"Do you accept this man as your lawfully wedded husband?" the priest asked.

"What? I guess so," Cortney mumbled, barely comprehending the situation.

And just like that, Cortney was married to Bill Gates. Her lifelong dream had been fulfilled, but it wasn't at all how she had imagined. She had always pictured a clear-minded, joyous ceremony, not a haze of champagne and confusion. Nevertheless, she was now Mrs. Gates, a reality that felt both surreal and unexpectedly anticlimactic.

Later that night, Courtney Love and Kurt Cobain were asleep, the tranquility of the night interrupted by the blaring of Bill Gates' house alarm across the lake.

Across the lake in Bill's house, Cortney carried her dog out of the bedroom door, setting off the alarm as she made her way to the yard. She got into her car, and Bill followed her with concern and surprise.

"Where are you going?" Bill asked with worry.

"I'm out of smokes and want to drink a bunch of Clearly Canadians. I'm so thirsty," Cortney replied.

"Ok. Are you coming back?" Bill asked awkwardly, as he tried to make sense of what was happening.

Cortney nodded in response, got into her car, and pulled away.

Cortney emerged from a 7-11 store, unwrapping a pack of cigarettes. She got into her car and lit one as the smoke curled around her face.

As she was driving on her way back, her cell phone rang. "Hello? Ok. I'm on my way," she said before ending the call.

Inside Kurt Cobain's abandoned apartment, he sat on the floor smoking, the dim light casted shadows on the walls. Cortney knocked on the door and entered, surprised to see him.

"Hey babe. I'm surprised you called me," Cortney said.

"No surprise. You have my cellular," Kurt replied.

"Yeah, I do. So why did you want to see me?" Cortney asked, sitting down next to him.

"Are you pregnant?" He asked in a direct and piercing tone.

"Not that I know of," Cortney answered, taken aback.

"Don't lie to me. Is it my baby?" Kurt demanded.

"There is no baby." Cortney said.

***

The next morning, Cortney and Daryl sat at the table, the weight of the conversation heavy in the air.

"What happened to your chin?" Daryl asked, noticing the bruise.

"I got drunk and ate the carpet. I'm pregnant with a drug addict's baby and want to marry a millionaire," Cortney confessed, her voice filled with frustration and despair. Under the influence of alcohol, she had forgotten about the previous night when she had already married Bill.

"You should really have this baby. If you marry, you should marry a man that will father the baby," Daryl advised.

"I don't want this baby. I want an abortion. Can you loan me the money?" Cortney pleaded, ignoring what her brother had said.

Daryl looked at her with concern and disapproval in his eyes. "Didn't you hear what I just said?" he asked.

      ***

Crowds of protestors gathered at the entrance of the abortion clinic, their signs and chants creating a tense atmosphere. Kurt Fenstad and Cortney pulled into the parking lot, the weight of the decision heavy on Cortney's mind.

Cortney looked out the window, her thoughts a swirling mix of anxiety and doubt.

This is Kurt's doing. How can I have his baby being married to Bill Gates? I don't know what Bill sees in me anyway. A high school dropout. An entertainer. The media would eat us alive. I'm 25 and I don't have medical insurance. And I really don't want to be connected to Kurt the rest of my life. She thought to herself.

Kurt glanced at her, "What?"

"Never mind. Let's go. I'm not going to fight these protestors," Cortney replied, her voice resigned as she took the decision to turn back for now.

Back at Kurt Fenstad's apartment, Cortney sat on the couch with her cat and dog, a bowl of popcorn in her lap. The TV flickered in the background as Kurt Fenstad walked through the living room.

"I'm off to hell," Kurt said, his tone casual.

"Super. Ciao," Cortney responded, barely looking up.

Kurt Fenstad left, and shortly after, Cortney's cell phone rang. Bill Gates' voice came through the line, "Hey, you haven't called or come over. Are you OK? Are we OK? Why didn't you come back the other night?"

"I'm sorry babe, but you know I'm scared of big dogs," Cortney explained, her voice softening. As she took the call, she rubbed her smooth chin casually, the carpet burns having already healed.

"You should have called. I've been worried." Bill's concern was evident.

"Yes, babe, we are more than OK. You're my other half. I've been thinking. Since you are allergic to Osiris, maybe we should buy a condo for me. You know Osiris isn't going to live forever, and it's a really good investment," Cortney suggested, picking up a real estate magazine. "There is a new development of condos. You would love it. I would love it," she added, flipping through the pages.

"Go take a look at them." Bill's voice was thoughtful.

Cortney sat back, the magazine open on her lap, contemplating the future. She felt the weight of her decisions, balancing her complicated life between Kurt Cobain and Bill Gates, and the prospect of a new beginning in a place of her own.

***

The next day, Cortney stood in the luxury condominium, the same real estate agent who had sold Kurt Cobain and Courtney Love their lake house now showing her around. The agent was animated, pointing out the high-end finishes and stunning views, but Cortney's mind was elsewhere. Her cell phone rang, pulling her from her thoughts.

"Hello," Cortney answered, her voice strained. "I'm sorry, Kurt, but I've lost the baby. All in all is all we are. I gotta go. I'm not alone, Kurt. Ciao."

She hung up the phone and tears welled up in her eyes, spilling over. The agent noticed her distress and approached with concern.

"Are you OK, Cortney?" the agent asked gently.

"No, I'm not," Cortney replied, wiping her tears. "I'm in love with Bill Gates and pregnant with Kurt Cobain's baby. No. I'm not OK."

The agent's eyes widened slightly. "Was that Kurt, Kurt Cobain you were on the phone with?"

"Yes," Cortney confirmed, sniffling. "Did you know him?"

"I know of him," the agent said, trying to stay professional despite her surprise. "Do you like the place?"

Cortney looked around, taking in the luxurious surroundings. "It's nice. It's in a perfect location by the Microsoft campus. I'll have Bill call you. He is buying it for me because he is allergic to my cat."

Cortney and the real estate agent walked out of the building, the bright daylight contrasting with the heaviness Cortney felt inside. They exchanged polite goodbyes before heading to their respective cars.

The agent sat in her car, pulling out her phone to make a call. She dialed quickly, her mind racing with the latest discoveries.

***

Back home, Cortney entered Kurt Fenstad's apartment, the familiarity of the place failing to soothe her nerves. The landline rang briefly, then stopped. Kurt Fenstad appeared from the bedroom, wearing only his underwear, carrying the portable phone.

"It's for you," Kurt said, handing the phone to her.

"Who is it?" Cortney asked, her heart sinking with curiosity and dread.

"It could be David," Kurt Fenstad replied with worry in his voice. "He has a Filipino accent."

"Hello?" Cortney took the phone reluctantly and replied.

"Hi, babe. I miss you. Do you miss me?" David Shaw's voice was frail, barely recognizable.

"Well, I'm happy you're alive," Cortney replied, trying to mask the turmoil inside her.

"Barely. I've got AIDS, babe. Come back to Los Angeles, and I'll get you the best doctors in the world to help you," David pleaded.

Cortney covered the phone with her hand and turned to Kurt Fenstad. "I've got AIDS," she whispered, her voice shaking.

Kurt's eyes widened in shock. "Hang up. Hang up the phone," he urged.

Ignoring him, Cortney continued the conversation. "Who shot you, David?"

"My brother was with me that night, and his gun went off. Please come back, babe. I'll buy you a home and..." David's voice trailed off.

"Don't ever call me again," Cortney interrupted, her voice resolute. She hung up and handed the phone back to Kurt Fenstad.

"Now you know he is alive," Kurt Fenstad said, trying to console her.

"But not well," Cortney muttered, the weight of the revelation pressing down on her.

"He is lying, Cort. He is manipulating you. I'm going to go back for another hour," Kurt said, heading back to bed.

"Sleep well," Cortney replied, forcing a weak smile.

She pulled out her cell phone and dialed a number. "Hey, babe, it's me. I really liked the condo. So you talked to the agent?"

Bill Gates sat in his living room as he answered the phone, the serene ambiance of his lake house contrasting sharply with the turmoil in Cortney's voice. "She said you told her we were engaged," Bill remarked with curiosity and concern.

"Yes, and that you were buying the place for

me," Cortney responded, her voice steady despite the chaos of the day.

Later that night, Kurt Cobain and Courtney Love stood at the window, looking across the lake at Bill Gates' house, where the lights glowed brightly against the night.

"I bought a car today," Courtney said, her voice breaking the silence. "Kurt, did you hear me? I bought a car today."

"What did you buy, Court?" Kurt turned to her, a curious look on his face.

"Come, let me show you." Courtney grabbed his hand excitedly.

Courtney walked behind Kurt, her hands covering his eyes. "Ready? Open your eyes," she said, removing her hands.

Kurt opened his eyes, his initial smile quickly turning to anger. "What the fuck is that yuppie piece of shit parked at my house for?" he demanded.

"It's a Lexus, Kurt," Courtney replied, her excitement dimming.

Kurt's face contorted with frustration. "No. Courtney Michelle Love, take it back."

They walked back into the house, tension thick in the air. Kurt grabbed a cigarette and lit it, taking a deep drag.

"People are starving in this world and dying," Kurt Cobain continued, his voice heavy with disdain. "And you want to drive an overpriced JAP car."

Courtney's eyes filled with frustration. "I don't want to ride around in a Volvo sedan anymore, Kurt."

"Take it back, Courtney. I mean it. I hate it for me, and I just hate it. I'm no way a yuppie. Take it back, or we are done," Kurt said in a firm tone of voice.

Courtney sighed, "Ok. I'll take it the fuck back," she muttered, turning away from him.

Chapter 8
Marilyn's Reincarnation

To be remembered is to live again through those who channel our spirit

Inside Bill's lake house, Cortney and Bill lay in bed, their bodies intertwined in the dim light. They kissed softly as their breaths mingled in the quiet room.

"Did you eat meat today?" Cortney asked, pulling back slightly to look into his eyes.

"No," Bill replied in a steady voice.

"I can taste it on your breath," Cortney insisted.

Bill Gates smiled slightly and leaned in closer. "Kiss me again," he whispered in a soft but seductive voice.

Cortney and Bill resumed their passionate embrace, their kisses growing deeper and more fervent. As their intimacy deepened, Cortney whispered, "Play something for us." Bill reached over to the nightstand and turned on the stereo, letting "Don't Let the Sun Go Down on Me" by George Michael play softly in the background, adding a tender touch to their moment.

The night outside was serene, the lake calm under the moonlight. Inside, the atmosphere was charged with a different kind of intensity. As they made love, the world outside faded away.

***

The next day at Bill Gates' office, the morning sun streamed through the large windows. Bill was on the phone, discussing business matters, when his secretary, Jane, entered the room. He quickly ended his call and looked up.

"Good morning, Bill," Jane greeted him with a warm smile.

"Good morning, Jane," Bill replied, returning the smile.

Jane hesitated for a moment before speaking. "Accounting called yesterday with charges on your credit card at a thrift store. Sir?"

"Yes. I know about the charges." Bill's expression remained calm.

"Really? You are shopping at a thrift store?" Jane looked slightly puzzled.

"Like I said, Jane, I know about the charges." Bill replied in a firm tone that was not unkind.

Jane nodded, accepting his response, though curiosity lingered in her eyes. She handed him a few documents and quietly left the room, leaving Bill to his thoughts.

Meanwhile at the Abortion Clinic, Cortney sat in the waiting room, her mind weighed down by the gravity of her decision. With trembling hands, she filled out the paperwork, carefully using Courtney Love's name and Bill Gates' credit card to pay. As she handed the paperwork to the receptionist, a sense of urgency filled the air.

The receptionist glanced at Cortney's form, then back at her. "Where is your ride?" she inquired with concern in her voice.

"I came in a cab. Could you call me one when I'm done with the procedure?" She pleaded with desperation evident in her tone and her heart pounding in her chest.

The receptionist shook her head slightly. "We really shouldn't," she said.

"Please, I really need to terminate this pregnancy. I've got AIDS and don't want to bring a sick child into the world," Cortney insisted.

The receptionist finally agreed and Cortney walked into the room to get her procedure done.

The clock on the wall ticked ominously, minutes passing by slowly. Finally, at 10 minutes to 3, Cortney emerged from the procedure, her movements sluggish from the anesthesia. She entered the lobby with her head still swimming.

The receptionist picked up the phone, her expression troubled. "Cortney, that's not your cab," she warned, her voice filled with concern.

Cortney looked out the window and saw a cab waiting. She stood up, still groggy.

"Cortney, that's not your cab," the receptionist repeated, a hint of alarm in her voice.

Cortney shook her head, dismissing the caution. "That's okay. I'll take this one. Thank you," she murmured, her voice barely above a whisper.

As she sat in the cab, Cortney Page handed the driver a piece of paper, her voice weary. "This is my home address and the directions," she said softly.

The cab driver took the paper without turning around. His silence was unsettling, but Cortney was too tired to care. She closed her eyes, hoping to find some relief in sleep. She didn't know how much time had passed when she was jolted awake. Disoriented, she felt herself being roughly dragged across the back seat. Panic set in as she realized what was happening.

She took a quick glance at the face of the man dragging her in the back seat of the cab, and a chill ran down her spine. He looked like Gary Ridgway. The full lips and mustache with beady eyes. Because she was still under the effects of the anesthesia, she couldn't tell if it was actually him or just a cab driver who looked like him. Her breath caught in her throat as the pieces fell into place. This could be the Green

River Killer.

Terror gripped her as she connected the dots. She tried to scream, but her voice came out as a strangled cry. The driver, now unmistakably resembling the notorious killer, moved with calculated cruelty. His eyes glinted with a malicious thrill as he tore off her bloody pad, a cruel sneer twisting his features. Cortney's mind raced, the horrific reality of her situation sinking in with each passing second. "No, please!" she screamed in a trembling voice. "I just had an abortion. Please, don't do this!"

The Cab driver's eyes glinted with malice. "Doesn't matter," he hissed, as his grip tightened.

Cortney's heart raced as she struggled, but her body was still weak from the procedure. The parking lot of Kurt's apartment building, empty and desolate, offered no sanctuary. Her pleas fell on deaf ears as the cab driver overpowered her.

Cortney screamed and her voice echoed in the confined space of the cab. The assault was brutal and relentless. Her body was still weak and dizzy, she couldn't muster the strength to fight back. As the Cab driver raped her, Cortney's resistance faded. She stopped fighting and her body went limp. She lay there as her mind retreated to a place where she could numb the pain. The horror of the moment was inescapable, but in her mind, she tried to distance herself from the violence inflicted upon her.

After he left, Cortney dragged herself up to Kurt's apartment. Once inside, she collapsed on the floor, her body shaking with sobs. She grabbed her phone and called Bill, crying hysterically.

"Bill, I... I need help," she managed to get out between sobs and tell Bill what had happened. "HE RAPED ME!" she yelled.

"Cortney, calm down. Knock on your neighbor's door for immediate help. I'm coming over right now," Bill instructed with urgency and concern.

Outside Kurt Fenstad's two-bedroom apartment, Cortney, bloodied and weak, knocked on her neighbor's door across the hall. As soon as she did, she collapsed at her own front door, her strength utterly spent.

The neighbor, alerted by the sound, opened her door and gasped at the sight. She rushed to Cortney's side, horrified by the blood covering her.

"Cortney! Cortney!" he cried, his voice rising in panic. "Help! Someone help!" she shouted, her eyes wide with fear as she looked around for assistance.

***

The following night at Seattle Hospital, Bill Gates sat by Cortney Page's bedside, his gaze filled with concern as she stirred awake in the dimly lit hospital room.

"Hi, babe. How are you feeling?" he asked softly.

Cortney's eyes fluttered open, confusion clouding her expression. "Where am I? Who are you?" she murmured.

As the nurse entered the room, she remarked, "There she is," addressing Cortney.

Cortney furrowed her brows in confusion. "What's happening?" she asked, her tone filled with unease.

The nurse proceeded to explain, "Your neighbor found you passed out in front of his door. This is your husband."

Cortney's disbelief was evident. "Is that true? This is like a cruel joke," she retorted in a shaky voice.

"I think I should leave now," Bill nodded, his heart heavy with the weight of the situation.

"Please do and don't come back," Cortney responded bitterly.

"Now, Cortney, don't be ugly to the man at your bedside. He's been here all day waiting for you to wake up." The nurse interjected gently.

"Just leave me alone," Cortney insisted.

As Bill rose to leave, he leaned over to kiss Cortney, but she recoiled, wiping it off with disdain.

With a heavy sigh, Bill exited the hospital room, followed closely by the nurse.

"You know she is lucky to be alive," the nurse said to Bill in a low voice, "She was raped after an abortion and has lost a lot of blood. She has a collapsed uterus, too, and will probably never be able to have children."

Bill's heart sank at the nurse's words. "Please don't tell her. I don't think she needs to know," he pleaded. "She doesn't seem to know what happened to her. To us."

"Amnesia," she added.

"How long does it take to get over?" Bill inquired in a low voice that was barely above a whisper.

"A few decades are what they say, but you never really get over amnesia," the nurse explained. "It's like Cortney's brain is like Swiss cheese. She'll have holes in her memory for the rest of her life."

Meanwhile, seizing the opportunity, Cortney quietly slipped out of her room, observing the backs of Bill and the nurse as they conversed. With a sense of detachment, she made her way to a nearby closet, where she put on a set of scrubs over her hospital gown.

In the lobby of Seattle Hospital, two receptionists sat at the front desk, their attention focused on their work. The elevator dinged, and Cortney stepped out, dressed in scrubs. She moved swiftly with footsteps that echoed in the quiet lobby, making sure she didn't catch any unwanted attention from the receptionists.

"I'm going for a smoke," she announced in a firm voice as she passed by the receptionists.

After successfully going outside Seattle Hospital, Cortney walked hastily behind the building towards University Village. Her pace quickened as the sound of alarms pierced the night. Her heart pounded with adrenaline and she broke into a run and dashed down the block to a nearby record store.

Cortney stood in line behind a couple of grunge guys, her eyes scanned the surroundings anxiously. When it was her turn, she approached the cashier.

"Do you have a phone I can use?" she asked, in a steady but urgent voice.

"Is it local?" the cashier responded, looking up from the register.

"Yes, the same area code," Cortney confirmed.

The cashier put the phone on the counter, and Cortney dialed quickly.

"Hi. It's me. Can you pick me up? I'm at the University Village's record store," she said into the receiver, with a trembling voice.

Shortly after, a Volvo sedan pulled up in front of the record store. Cortney quickly got in, the driver remaining unseen in the darkness.

"You're the only number I could remember," Cortney began, her voice filled with both relief and confusion. "I woke up in the hospital with a stranger saying he was my husband. I don't remember. The nurse said I collapsed and had lost a lot of blood."

"I really think I should take you back to the hospital," Kurt Fenstad's voice came from the driver's seat.

"No. Please take me home," Cortney pleaded. "I promise I'll never tell a soul you helped me. I will never think about this moment, so I guarantee you I'll forget it, and you should, too," she insisted with desperation.

***

The next day, in the GM Electric office, Cortney stood at the copier machine, a small puddle of blood forming at her feet. Alarmed, she made her way to the hallway and approached an office door.

"I'm having a gusher of a period. I've got to go home. Can you sign me out?" she asked urgently in embarrassment and distress.

Later that night, in Kurt Fenstad's apartment, Cortney emerged from the bathroom. Kurt was sitting on the edge of the bed, putting on his shoes.

"Don't go to work," Cortney pleaded, her eyes wide with a mix of desperation and excitement. "Better yet, quit your job. Move to LA with me. I'll go back to doing singing telegrams, and we can work background in movies for money. Even better, you can be my photographer and we can take pictures with the tourists. I once dated this guy that used to dress up in a chicken suit for El Pollo Loco. He told me I should go to Hollywood Boulevard and pose for tips. I need you to quit your job at Boeing and move to Hollywood."

Kurt looked up as a broad smile spread across his face. "You know that is the craziest idea you've ever had."

"So, is that a yes?" Cortney asked with eyes full of hope.

"Yes!"

***

It was a bright day outside Mann's Chinese Theater. The song "I'm Too Sexy" by Right Said Fred played from one of the tour buses, adding to the lively atmosphere. Tour buses came and went, unloading hundreds of Asian tourists with cameras ready. Cortney Page and Kurt Fenstad were back in LA and back in business.

Cortney Page stood among them, using a fan

to hide her face from all the photos being taken. Next to her, Kurt Fenstad wore a hat with a sign that said "$5.00" and held a Polaroid camera. People lined up to have their picture taken with Cortney.

"My feet are killing me," Cortney said, shifting her weight.

"We've made a few hundred dollars. Let's go," Kurt Fenstad said after looking at the cash they had made.

Cortney and Kurt walked to their car, counting the money. As they passed the Hollywood Roosevelt Hotel, they saw a sign in the window for a Marilyn Monroe lookalike contest.

"You are a dead ringer for Marilyn," A man nearby noticed Cortney and he said.

"Thank you," She replied with a smile.

The man pointed to the sign. "If you win, you'll be cast in a feature film. That's what the ad says."

Cortney glanced at the sign being doubtful. "Yeah, it's probably a publicity stunt for the film," she said.

"You should enter. I'll be here looking for ya," the man replied.

Cortney smiled and nodded as they continued on their way, the sun setting behind them.

The next day at Marina del Rey Beach. Cortney Page lay on a beach towel, soaking up the sun, while Kurt Fenstad swam in the ocean. They were enjoying the California coast and the freedom of their unconventional lifestyle.

Cortney's thoughts wandered as she thought to herself, Being Marilyn makes a lot of people happy, and I'm happy making rent. A lot of Asians believe that I am Marilyn reincarnated. Kurt emerged from the waves and approached her towel, water dripping from his hair.

"You got to go in the water," Kurt said, shaking off the saltwater.

"No thanks, sharks love me," Cortney replied with a smirk.

"Are you on your period?" Kurt raised an eyebrow.

"That's a personal question. I'm booked on a movie set tomorrow and will be going downtown. I get booked wearing my red wig. No one wants a blonde background extra." Cortney said with a frown.

Kurt chuckled, stretching out on the sand beside her. "Blondes are leading ladies, my dear. People always look at a blonde's face when driving down the street. The eye naturally goes to the light hair color first. No one wants to be upstaged in looks, and that, my dear, is your double-edged sword—being blonde and beautiful."

"And what are you saying, cousin?" Cortney rolled her eyes.

"You're a leading lady type, and you've been typecast as Marilyn. That's why Playboy didn't want your image. You can't be famous as Marilyn. You must be famous as Cortney Page."

Cortney sighed, staring out at the ocean. "I don't really want to be an actress. I want to be a personality. I just want to stay home in my pajamas, smoke pot all day, and get paid for it. That's my dream job." She giggled at the thought.

"How do you plan to get paid?" Kurt laughed.

"I'm going to design a pay-per-minute software and be a life coach. I've got new business cards. Look," Cortney said, handing Kurt a business card. The card had a black and white picture of her with Goddess Isis and the number 855-X2C-4U2C on it. She lit a joint, the spark catching the light on her engagement ring, and passed it to Kurt.

"I also have a singing telegram gig," Cortney added, taking a puff.

"Do you want me to drive you?" Kurt asked, exhaling smoke.

"No. I've got a driver picking up other girls and me. Hi-O-Sylver booked it," she replied.

"Isn't she the famous stripper from the radio?" Kurt asked, taking another hit from the joint.

"The one and the same," Cortney confirmed with a smile, enjoying the warm beach breeze.

***

The next day, Cortney Page drove into the parking lot of a bustling movie set in downtown Los Angeles. She wore a long red-haired wig, ready for her role. The block was filled with trucks, security guards, and catering tents with tables and chairs set up for the crew.

Inside the set, the crew was busy filming. Cortney walked through an office set, swinging a shopping bag. She wore cat-eye glasses and carried a Chanel purse.

"That's a wrap for lunch," the director called out, signaling a break.

Cortney made her way to the back of the set, where Harvey Weinstein stood. As she passed, Harvey reached out and took her left hand.

"Do you work? Because with a tan like yours, you look independently wealthy," Harvey said, a sly smile on his face.

"I'm a street performer. I work for myself," Cortney replied coolly.

"Why don't you come to my hotel tonight, and we'll discuss getting you some real work as an actress." Harvey said.

"Sure, I'll bring my strap-on and fuck the shit out of you, literally and figuratively." Cortney gave an immediate and sharp response.

The nearby crew and grips snickered, enjoying the exchange.

Harvey's face darkened. "I'm the sheriff in this town," he said menacingly.

"Meet your new sheriff," Cortney shot back, walking away without a second glance.

As she left, Harvey waved over Betty, the wardrobe girl. "Who's her fiancé?" he demanded.

"Brandon Lee," Betty answered simply.

Outside, the crew and background extras were gathered, eating lunch. Cortney stood in line, waiting for her turn. A grip walked by with his food tray, nodding in her direction.

"There she is, Cowboy," he said, acknowledging her with a grin.

Chapter 9
Have We Met Before?

Every stranger is just a friend we haven't met yet, or perhaps met long ago

Cortney Page stood at the door of Dina's condo in Santa Monica, feeling a light breeze from the ocean. Dina opened the door with a welcoming smile and let her in. Inside, a little boy sat at the table, deeply engrossed in coloring.

Dina handed Cortney a Vanity Fair Magazine, opened to an article featuring Courtney Love, who was pregnant and married to Kurt Cobain.

"Look. It's Courtney and Kurt," Dina said, pointing to the glossy photos.

Cortney glanced at the page. "I know this couple," she said slowly.

"You know Courtney Love and Kurt Cobain?" Dina looked surprised.

"I think so. But I really don't remember," Cortney replied, her brow furrowing as she tried to recall.

"What happened to you in Seattle?" Dina

asked in a tone filled with curiosity.

Cortney sighed. "Like I've said before, I woke up in the hospital unable to remember anything but a phone number to get picked up."

"Whose phone number?" Dina inquired.

"Kurt's," Cortney answered.

"Your cousin, Kurt, or Kurt Cobain?" Dina asked further.

Cortney shook her head in frustration, "I really don't remember, Dina."

"They're having a baby and are using heroin." Dina glanced back at the magazine.

"Well, I've never done heroin, so I don't know how I would know them," Cortney said in a defensive tone.

"Where's Alexander? Alexander?!" Dina's attention shifted suddenly.

The toilet flushed, and the bathroom door opened. A young boy named Alexander emerged.

"You know, Gary rescued Alexander from the roof. He was walking on the ledge of the building," Dina said with equal amounts of worry and relief in her voice.

"Well, he is Steve Olson's son. He was born with good balance because his father is a famous skateboarder." Cortney managed a small smile.

Dina raised an eyebrow. "What's Gary's story, then? He had better balance getting my son down in one piece."

"You know what?" Cortney paused.

"What?" Dina looked at her expectantly.

"Never mind," Cortney said, shaking her head as if to clear away the confusion and memories she couldn't quite grasp.

Inside Cortney's one-bedroom house in Culver City, her dog and cat greeted her eagerly as she entered the dimly lit room. It was nighttime, and the soft glow of lamps created a warm ambiance. She walked over to her desk in the dining room, noticing the blinking light on her answering machine.

"Hi Cortney, this is Owen Hamblutzal III, and I'm directing a student film here at USC. I saw your headshot in the school office and want to cast you in my movie. Call me at 213-555-8828. Thanks, Owen," the answering machine announced.

Cortney grabbed a pen and quickly jotted down the number. She picked up her portable phone and dialed Owen's number.

"Hi, this is Cortney Page... 'The Blood Clot,' huh? Sounds interesting," she said as she pressed the speakerphone button.

Owen's voice came through the speaker, slightly muffled. "The movie is about you finding a blob of blood and mothering it to become a young child. What is your experience?"

Cortney leaned back in her chair, considering her response. "I've done a lot of theater and stage performances as Marilyn Monroe. I do have a sizzle reel, so I'd be happy to do it."

The desert sun beat down relentlessly on the crew of four guys in Palmdale Desert. Owen, along with three others, stood by their cars, preparing for the day's shoot. Kurt Fenstad pulled up, driving Cortney to the set. They greeted the crew with handshakes as they all stepped out of their vehicles.

Inside the movie car, Cortney sat, tears streaming down her face, and chain-smoking as the ashtray filled with cigarette butts.

Outside, in the Palmdale Desert, Owen sat in the passenger seat of a second car, filming as Adam drove alongside Cortney's vehicle. They eventually pulled over, and Owen voiced his concern.

"Are you okay?" Owen asked with genuine worry.

"I'm fine. I was just thinking about my childhood dog. It always makes me cry," Cortney replied, being a little sentimental.

"You really fooled us. You are very good at acting. We are done for the day," Owen said, impressed by Cortney's performance.

Later that night, in Cortney's Culver City one-bedroom house, she sat in the fenced-in front yard with her dog and cat on a leash. She smoked a joint as the phone rang inside the house. Cortney went inside, grabbed her portable phone, and took it outside with her.

In the dim light of the night, Cortney continued smoking her joint as she answered the call.

"Hello. Oh, hi, Owen," Cortney greeted the caller. "Oh really? And the baby's name again? Bean for a name. That's odd. And what's up with the Francis Farmer name? Well, they are very strange people. Anyway, thanks for thinking of me and calling. OK, Ciao'."

She hung up the phone, exhaling smoke into the cool night air, her thoughts drifting momentarily to the eccentricities of Hollywood before she returned her attention to the peaceful night around her.

***

The morning sun streamed brightly through the windows of Wally George's Studios. Inside, Wally and Cortney stood on stage, radiating in natural daylight. A small crew moved around them, cameras ready to capture every moment.

"So, Marilyn, is it OK to call you Marilyn?" Wally asked with a grin.

"They all do," Cortney replied, smiling back.

"I met Marilyn at the Brown Derby," Wally reminisced.

Later that night, in the D.C. Marriott Penthouse, an Arab man named Golem Mohammed, dressed in his prayer robe watched TV intently, just then Cortney's voice caught his attention.

"So you met me before," Cortney's voice echoed from the television.

"This is the first time I've met you," Wally's voice replied.

"It's the first time you met Cortney, but the second time you met me as Marilyn. I'm her. We have the mirrored reflection birthmarks," Cortney explained.

"That's very interesting. Tell our audience how they can get a hold of you," Wally prompted.

"They can call the Ron Smith Celebrity Look Alike Agency in Hollywood," Cortney answered confidently.

As the TV continued to play in the background, Golem Mohammed picked up the phone beside him and dialed 411, speaking in an Arabian accent.

"Can I get the telephone number for the Ron Smith Celebrity Look Alike Agency in Hollywood, California?" he requested.

Later that night, inside the dimly lit USC Theater at night, Cortney's black and white film, "The Blob," played on screen. The film showed her emoting intensely, surrounded by a cluttered ashtray filled with stubbed-out cigarettes. Cortney sat beside Owen and Kurt Fenstad, absorbed in the screening.

"This came out really well. You really should stick to acting," Kurt remarked.

"My acting agent hasn't called me in a long time," Cortney admitted softly.

The audience hushed as the theater lights suddenly brightened, signaling the end of the film and the MC took the stage.

"That was 'The Blob' by Owen Hamblutzal III. Owen," the MC announced.

Owen stood and approached the microphone. "I'd like to thank my fellow students and crew, and especially our actress, Cortney Page," he expressed gratefully.

Cortney stood briefly, waved to the crowd, and then sat back down. Only Kurt Fenstad's applause rang out in the theater.

***

Inside the Ron Smith Look Alike Agency office during the day, receptionist Nikki was busy faxing copies of Cortney's headshot to various contacts.

Meanwhile, outside the Larry Flynt Building in daylight, a limousine pulled up. Cortney stepped out accompanied by a man and woman and entered the building. A man behind the desk handed them a stack of DVD and CD copies and the trio was on the bustling streets of Los Angeles, the limousine drove through traffic and Cortney handed out CDs to various people they encountered along the way, pausing briefly each time before returning to the limo.

"OK, that's the last of the disks," Cortney announced, relieved to be done with their distribution task for the day.

As the night sky enveloped the surroundings outside the Rose Bowl, Cortney and Kurt Fenstad mingled at the Guns N' Roses and Metallica backstage party. Cortney took pictures with various guests, capturing moments of laughter and celebration. Suddenly, Axl Rose entered the scene, drawing attention as he moved through the crowd. Cortney started walking towards him, but was intercepted by Axl's brother, Stewart.

"Cortney Page, you were hand-picked by my brother for tonight's party," Stewart greeted her.

"Oh, yeah? Why me and not Stephanie

Anderson?" Cortney asked curiously.

"Because you're Kurt's girlfriend," Stewart replied knowingly.

"Kurt's my cousin," Cortney corrected him.

"Not that Kurt. Here he comes," Stewart clarified.

With Axl Rose, 1992

Axl Rose approached them, and Cortney posed for a picture with the rock legend, while Kurt Fenstad snapped the photo. This picture later found its place on the wall of Cortney's home, serving as a cherished memento of that unforgettable night at the Rose Bowl party.

With award season in full swing, the MTV Awards were a spectacle of music and glamour. Inside the vibrant atmosphere of the event, Nirvana's electrifying performance of "Lithium" reached its climax. Kurt Cobain lost it, his passion overtaking him as he poked his guitar into one of the speakers behind and eventually threw it across the stage towards the back where the band was seated. Then, he climbed on the speakers and fell onto the drums, creating chaos and excitement in the crowd.

As the song ended, the grunge sounds of the guitar echoed through the venue, mingling with David Grohl's playful banter, adding a wild touch to the performance.

"Hi, Axl. Hi, Axl. Where's Axl? Hi, Axl," David Grohl exclaimed, injecting a bit of humor into the intense musical moment.

***

Back at Cortney's cozy Culver City one-bedroom house during the day, she was meticulously dressed as Marilyn Monroe when Kurt Fenstad walked in.

"Hi Cort. Are you ready?" Kurt greeted her.

"Ready as I'll ever be," Cortney replied with a smile.

"Where's your suitcase?" Kurt asked, glancing around.

"I'm flying in and out today. This rich Saudi Arabian is meeting me at the airport," Cortney explained.

"Another Ron Smith gig?" Kurt inquired knowingly.

"Yep," Cortney affirmed, preparing for another adventure in her career as a Marilyn Monroe look-alike.

Under the bright midday sun, Cortney stepped out of Kurt's car at Los Angeles Airport. With a quick wave, she made her way into the bustling terminal, ready for her latest gig. Hours later, as the night sky wrapped around the city, she emerged from the terminal, tired but satisfied, and climbed back into Kurt Fenstad's car.

Back at her cozy one-bedroom house in Culver City, Cortney was dressed in a dazzling hot pink Marilyn Monroe dress, complete with sparkling rhinestone jewelry. Her dog and cat, each on a leash, waited in the fenced-in front yard. Cortney opened the door and called out, "Come on, guys. Time to come in."

As her pets trotted inside, a knock sounded at the back door. Surprised, Cortney peered through the door window and saw Brad Pitt standing there with two stripper girls. She opened the door wide as her curiosity piqued.

"Please come in. I'm Cortney Page," she greeted them warmly.

"I'm Billy, and this is Candy and Lola," Brad Pitt introduced with a charming smile on his face.

The girls disappeared into the bathroom while Brad Pitt wandered around the room, admiring the pictures of Cortney with Axl Rose, Billy Idol, and various pieces of Marilyn Monroe artwork.

With Billy Idol, 1992

"Who's the artist?" Brad asked, his eyes lingering on a particularly striking piece.

"Me," Cortney replied with pride. Then, with a playful grin, she added, "You know, you are a really good-looking man."

Cortney's mind drifted as she narrated internally, Little did I know that we had slept together before I moved to Seattle. It was 1987, and I went out with Jason Priestley, and we brought our roommates.

***

On a warm summer night in Venice Beach, 22-year-old Cortney found herself in her townhouse kitchen, rolling a joint. Suddenly, there was a knock at the door. Opening it, she was surprised to find Jason Priestley, just 18 years old, and Brad Pitt, who was 23, standing outside.

At Jason's Book signing event, 2014

"Hi, guys. Come in. I was just rolling a joint," Cortney said, inviting them inside. She called upstairs, "Tori, come on down. Jason and…" She paused, glancing at Brad, "I'm sorry, what's your name again?"

"Bill, short for William," Brad replied.

"And William is here," Cortney finished. Tori came downstairs, and Cortney lit the joint, passing it to her. Tori took a deep inhale before handing it to Jason.

"Tori, this is Jason and William," Cortney

introduced.

"Hi. Want some?" Tori offered the joint.

"No thanks. I'm driving." Jason shook his head.

"An Aston Martin." Brad grinned.

"How old are you?" Cortney looked at him and asked with intrigue.

"He's 18, and I'm 23. I'll be 24 in December." Brad answered for both of them.

"Sagittarius or Capricorn?" Cortney asked.

"That's such a typical pick-up line. What's your sign?" Tori asked, giving out a chuckle.

"I'm a Sagittarius." Brad replied.

"I'm a Pisces. I was born on President's Day. And what about you, Jason? What is your sign?" Cortney asked with a grin.

"Virgo," Jason said simply.

Cortney's eyes lit up. "Pisces and Sagittarius used to share the same planet until Neptune was discovered. Then Pisces moved to Neptune. Sagittarius maintained Jupiter, the planet of luck and fortune. Virgos are my direct opposite."

"Opposite. So there's no hope for us?" Jason asked with intrigue.

Cortney shook her head with a playful smile. "Opposites attract, so Virgo and Pisces are the best match." Brad took a hit from the joint and passed it back to Cortney.

As the conversation continued, Cortney found herself increasingly drawn to Brad, sensing an undeniable chemistry. They exchanged glances and flirtatious remarks, the air was thick with tension.

Later that night, Cortney stepped out of the bathroom, wearing a tie-dye T-shirt with a smiling face that read "Don't Worry, Be Happy." She had no pants on and as she stepped out she saw Brad Pitt lying naked, comfortably on her bed that had a fur blanket over it.

Brad looked at her with mischievous eyes. "What's your favorite perfume?" he asked.

Cortney smiled, walking towards the bed. "The only perfume," she replied.

"What's that?" Brad Asked.

"Chanel No. 5. My grandmother says that only ladies wear it. So, it's stuck in my head. That's why I only wear Chanel No. 5."

"Come here." Brad said.

Cortney jumped into bed and they began to kiss passionately. Brad turned her over, laying on top of her back.

"Relax, let me put it in here. Just relax," Brad whispered.

Cortney moaned until her breath hitched. "Yes, yes. Oh my god! I love it. I love you." She reached her climax, then turned over and kissed Brad deeply.

Brad looked into her eyes, "Only married couples do that together. Don't ever do that with anyone but me. Cortney, promise me." He said.

"Are you saying we are married?"

"Promise me. It's mine," Brad insisted.

"I promise." She replied.

"If not, when you least expect it, expect it."

"Is that a threat?" Cortney asked.

I switched dates that night and took William home instead of Jason. William and I had sex everywhere that night. On the stairs, the sofa, the bed, and the shower. We were fucking when there were earthquakes, and William sped up the humping and didn't let me jump up to stand in a doorway.

Cortney drove Brad Pitt down the sunlit streets of West Hollywood, the warm California breeze ruffling her hair. She pulled up in front of Jason Priestley's apartment and glanced at Brad, who looked curious.

"My friend, Linda Kerkorian, lives across the

street," Cortney said, pointing. "She was at the club last night — the girl driving the Porsche."

"Who is that?" Brad asked.

"She's the daughter of Kirk Kerkorian, the owner of MGM Studios, hotels, and everything MGM. Kirk Kerkorian runs this town."

"Give me your number." He asked Cortney out of the blue.

Cortney hesitated, then reached into her glove compartment, pulling out a piece of paper. She scribbled a fake number and handed it to him.

I gave him the wrong number because I didn't feel right going around Jason's back. He was my date. Jason had my number, so I guess I made a frenemy.

"Thanks, Cortney." Brad replied with a smile as he took the paper, oblivious to her inner conflict.

She forced a smile back, hoping she made the right decision.

Chapter 10
Another Bad Decision

Every detour has its own lessons.

Inside Cortney's one-bedroom house in Culver City, Brad Pitt, now 28, admired the art adorning the walls. Candy and Lola emerged from another room and settled on the sofa.

"You've got talent," Brad said, studying a particularly striking piece.

"And you've got great looks," Cortney replied with a smile. "You need to be a movie star. I would pay $15 to see a film you starred in. I'm taking acting classes at the Actor's Studio. You should come by. I've also got an agent who represents Sharon Stone. As a matter of fact, I've got a meeting this week with Chuck Binder."

Brad looked intrigued. "I'll drive you there. Hi O Slyver has my number."

Cortney handed him a business card featuring a black and white picture of herself labeled "Goddess Isis" with an 800 number. "Here's my card. My agent is in the same building as the Ron Smith Celebrity Lookalike Agency, my other agent, and how I met Chuck Binder. They're in the old Pure Platinum nightclub building on Hollywood and Vine. My stomping grounds where I've made a good living as a Marilyn Monroe impersonator."

"It's a date. OK, girls, let's get going. We don't want to be late." Brad said with a smile.

Later that night, Brad Pitt drove his Jeep through the busy streets of Los Angeles with Cortney seated behind him. He frequently glanced at her reflection in the rearview mirror, unable to hide his fascination.

They arrived at a vibrant Japanese nightclub. The neon lights cast a colorful glow on the sidewalk as everyone got out of the car. Brad opened Cortney's door with a chivalrous gesture, and they all entered the club together, with Brad holding the door open for the girls.

The atmosphere inside was lively, filled with music and laughter. Cortney couldn't help but think back to their earlier conversation about acting and the possibilities that lay ahead. She felt a mix of excitement and nostalgia, wondering if this night was the start of something new or simply another chapter in her life.

In the dimly lit dressing room of the Japanese nightclub, Brad Pitt sat at a small table, carefully counting piles of cash. The girls, Candy and Lola, were standing around him, taking out crumpled bills from their tops and panties, and adding them to the growing stack.

"OK," Brad said, separating the money into neat piles. "I keep $200, and you girls get $150 each plus whatever Hi O Slyver pays you."

He opened the door, ready to leave, but paused when he saw Cortney standing there, trying to discreetly stuff a dollar bill into her glove.

"Keep your dollar," Brad said with a grin, catching her in the act.

Cortney blushed and laughed, tucking the dollar away. "Just trying to make an honest living," she said with a wink.

"You're something else, Cortney."

***

The next day, Brad Pitt's Jeep was parked outside Cortney's cozy one-bedroom house in Culver City. In the fenced-in front yard, Cortney and Brad sat comfortably, her dog and cat leashed nearby. They passed a joint back and forth as they enjoyed the relaxed atmosphere of the sunny day.

"Let's go meet our agent," Cortney said, exhaling a plume of smoke.

"Let's go." Brad nodded.

"Are you okay to drive?" she asked.

"Yes, I'm okay to drive. Don't worry your pretty little head." Brad smiled reassuringly.

After a short car ride, Cortney and Brad walked into the waiting room of their agent's office, the walls covered with posters of past clients and successful projects. The receptionist, busy on the phone, glanced up as they entered. She quickly finished her call and smiled at them.

"I'm here for Chuck," Cortney said.

"I'll let him know. Please have a seat." The receptionist nodded.

Cortney and Brad settled on the sofa together. Brad put his arm around her, but the gesture felt awkward, the tension of the upcoming meeting was tense between them.

A few moments later, the receptionist looked up. "Cortney, Chuck will see you now. And he'll see your friend after."

Brad stood up with a confident smile. "Brad Pitt."

"Brad?" Cortney looked at him, slightly taken aback

Years earlier, in the intimacy of her Venice Beach townhouse, Cortney, and Brad Pitt, lay in bed together. The moonlight filtered through the curtains making the room alight in a soft glow.

"What's your last name?" Cortney turned to Brad and asked.

"Pitt."

"Willy Pitt is a terrible name. What about your middle name?"

"Bradley."

"Brad is one of my favorite baby names. You should go by Brad Pitt."

"You think so?"

"Absolutely."

With a sudden jerk from Cortney Brad came back to the present after reminiscing this sudden memory.

"Brad?" Cortney said.

"Yeah, Brad Pitt." Brad nodded.

"I'll be going in first and you can come after me, alright?" She explained.

"Alright." He said.

The clock on the wall showed 3 p.m. as Cortney stepped into Chuck Binder's office. The room felt professional, with sleek furniture and posters of Hollywood stars on the walls. The smell of polished wood, leather, and a hint of coffee filled the air.

Fifteen minutes later, Cortney came out of the office, her face showed a mix of anticipation and calm. She gave Brad a reassuring nod before he stood up and made his way into the office. The waiting room was quiet, the only sound being the tik-tok of the clock and the murmur of the receptionist on a phone call.

Inside the office, Brad took a seat across from Chuck, who eyed him with a curiosity.

"Cortney gave you rave reviews," Chuck began, leaning back in his chair. "Are you working now?"

"I'm working on getting an agent. I like you,

Chuck, and I know you represent some of the greats like me." Brad met his gaze and said with a confident smile.

"My roster is pretty full, and I'm not taking new people now." Chuck sighed, looking at the stack of headshots and resumes on his desk.

"Then drop Cortney and let Ron Smith make his fortune. Sign me, and I'll make you a fortune. Cortney has been typecast as Marilyn Monroe, Chuck. She looks just like her." He said cunningly.

There was a moment of silence as Chuck considered Brad's words. He looked down at his desk, tapping his fingers thoughtfully before reaching out to shake Brad's hand.

"You know, you are right," Chuck said, "We've got a deal."

"Thank you, Chuck. You won't regret this."

***

Brad Pitt's Jeep pulled up in front of Cortney's house. As the engine idled, Cortney unfastened her seatbelt and turned to Brad.

"Thanks for the ride, Brad," she said with a smile, waving goodbye as she stepped out.

"Anytime, Cortney. See you soon." Brad nodded, watching as she made her way to the back door.

Cortney waved one last time before slipping through the back door into her kitchen.

Inside, the house was quiet and still. Cortney's dog and cat greeted her with love. She petted them both affectionately before moving to the answering machine, pressing play curiously.

"Hi, Cortney. This is Nikki from the Ron Smith Celebrity Lookalike Agency. Penny Marshall was at that Marilyn Monroe lookalike contest you entered—the one Stephanie Anderson won. She wants to cast you as the voice of Marilyn, with Stephanie as Marilyn's body double. Please call me as soon as you get this message. I'll be here until 6 o'clock. Bye, bye."

Cortney's heart raced as she listened to the message. Glancing at her watch, she saw it was exactly 6 p.m. She quickly dialed the number. The phone barely rang once before Nikki picked up.

"Ron Smith Celebrity Lookalike Agency. This is Nikki. How can I help you?"

"Oh, good. You're still there," Cortney said with a sense of relief.

"Yes, Cortney. Glad you got back to me. So, you got my message. Do you want to audition?"

"I'm there," Cortney replied without hesitation.

"Wait a minute," Nikki interjected. "It's about three young men who go to Hollywood to meet Marilyn. It stars Jason Priestley. You still want to do it?"

Cortney paused for a brief moment, but her resolve was firm. "Yes. I want to do it."

"Great! We'll set up a time for you. Talk to you soon." Nikki's voice brightened.

Cortney hung up the phone as excitement and nostalgia washed over her. She was ready to seize this opportunity, no matter what it entailed. With determination, she began to prepare for the audition, knowing that this could be the break she had been waiting for.

It was the next day and Kurt Fenstad navigated the bustling Sony Pictures Studio lot, driving Cortney through the various sets and soundstages. They finally parked near Penny Marshall's studio office.

Cortney and Kurt entered the waiting room, where anticipation flowed in the air like an electric current.

"Break a leg," Kurt encouraged with a supportive smile.

"I don't need to break a leg. I've got the role," Cortney said confidently. "This is just a formality."

An Assistant emerged from Penny Marshall's office with a clipboard in hand.

"Cortney Page? Penny Marshall will see you now," the Assistant announced.

Cortney nodded, her heart fluttered with excitement as she followed the Assistant into Penny Marshall's office. The door closed behind her, leaving Kurt waiting outside.

***

Later that evening, Cortney sat at her dining room table, skillfully sewing gowns. Her phone rang on the nearby desk, and she answered it casually.

"Hello? Oh, hi Dina. Right now? Courtney Love is on the radio? OK, I'll turn it on. Thanks for telling me. Bye."

Cortney, now 29 years old, stepped out from her house in pajamas, her dog in tow. She climbed into her car and switched on the radio. The radio broadcast continued with the DJ and Courtney Love's voice echoing through the car speakers.

No. I'm a Cancer, Kurt's old girlfriend was the Pisces. He says he got along better with her than me, but she was crazy.

Where is Kurt tonight?

He's actually doing a charity concert tonight at the Whiskey a Go Go.

Cortney started her car with a determined face. "OK, Gioia," she spoke to her dog, steeling herself for what lay ahead. "We're going to face my fear and go talk to this Kurt Cobain guy myself. We're going to get to the bottom of this."

With a resolute nod, Cortney pulled out of her driveway, her destination set: the Whiskey a Go Go.

After arriving at the club, Cortney parked her car under the glow of streetlights near the busty entrance of the Whiskey a Go Go club. Dressed in pajamas and slippers, she left her dog safely inside and approached Vince Vaughan, an approximately 22 year-old doorman stationed at the entrance.

"Are you on the list?" Vince asked as he inspected her driver's license.

"I know Kurt Cobain. Well, I think I might know him," Cortney replied with uncertainty.

"What do you mean you think you might know him?" Vince inquired out of curiosity.

"It's a long story, but I used to live in Seattle. I lost my memory. I read a Vanity Fair article a few years ago, and when I saw their picture, I knew them but didn't know how," Cortney explained, hoping to clarify.

"Go on in, Miss Cortney Page," Vince said, nodding slightly.

"Thanks, I won't be long," Cortney thanked him and entered the club, where the music and chatter enveloped her senses. Sometime later, she exited with her thoughts swirling with fragments of conversation and forgotten memories.

"What did he say?" Vince asked, curious about her interaction inside.

"He said I had his abortion to marry Bill Gates. I vanished from their Seattle music scene after I was raped," Cortney recounted, her voice full of disbelief.

"Rape Me," Vince remarked.

"What?" Cortney was puzzled.

"Nirvana's song, 'Rape Me,'" Vince clarified.

"I don't know it. I listen to the WAVE," Cortney admitted, trying to make sense of the connection.

"Yeah, I know the new age radio station," Vince acknowledged.

"Well, thanks. I appreciate you believing me and that I'm not some crazed fan wanting to pull a Rebecca Schaeffer on him," Cortney said gratefully.

With that, she walked back to her car, her mind raced with unanswered questions about her past and the connections she was starting to unravel.

Back in the club, Nirvana's raw energy reverberated through the crowded nightclub. On stage, Kurt Cobain abruptly stopped playing and approached the microphone, his presence commanded the room.

"You know Cortney is the best fuck I've ever had. I'm in love with a goddess," Kurt announced.

Meanwhile, Cortney sat in her car, tears streamed down her face as she struggled to comprehend Kurt's unexpected declaration.

"Why? Why me?" she cried out in anguish, her emotions overwhelmed her.

***

In the peaceful courtyard of the Marina Del Ray rehab center, Kurt Cobain stood alone, smoking a cigarette. The peaceful atmosphere was interrupted by an orderly's voice.

"Kurt, you've got a visitor," the orderly informed him.

Cortney Page walked into the courtyard, stirring a range of emotions in Kurt's expression.

"Hi, Kurt. How are you? How did you end up in this place?" Cortney greeted him gently, trying to make sense of the situation.

"Thank you for coming," Kurt replied sincerely.

"I signed in as Minnie Mouse. If I signed Mickey Mouse, I would be declaring war," Cortney joked lightly, trying to ease the tension.

"Funny," Kurt chuckled softly. "Look, Cortney, I want things to go back to the way they were with us."

"I wish I could help you, but I really don't remember an 'us.' I showed up at your concert to try and piece my memories together," Cortney confessed in a sad voice.

"I'm divorcing Courtney. Come with me to Seattle," Kurt pleaded earnestly.

"OK," Cortney agreed, unsure but willing to take a leap of faith.

"Really? You'll make me so happy. Now let me climb on your back to scale this wall," Kurt said eagerly, his spirit lifting.

"OK. You shouldn't be in this place anyway," Cortney replied, bending over as Kurt climbed onto her back and together, they scaled the wall, leaving behind the confines of the rehab center.

***

Cortney sat in her car, parked in front of the terminal of Los Angeles airport. She watched as Kurt Cobain emerged, holding two tickets. Kurt climbed into the passenger seat beside her.

"OK. Now park the car in the lot. I got us first-class tickets home," Kurt said eagerly.

"I can't go, Kurt," Cortney replied softly. "I know I said I would, and I may have loved you, but you're a familiar stranger to me now. I don't know you."

"Yes, you know me. You knew me before I was famous. You introduced me to my wife; soon-to-be-ex-wife. You got us played on the radio," Kurt insisted.

"I'm sorry, Kurt. Plus, I've got an acting audition on Tuesday for a television series called 'Friends.' This could be my big break. I don't want to miss the opportunity," Cortney explained.

"What are you playing? The voices in their heads?" Kurt asked sarcastically. "I'll come back then. I'll go to Seattle and return next week."

"I'll date you, but I can't promise you that things will be the way they used to be because I don't remember how they were," Cortney said.

Kurt pulled Cortney closer and then kissed her passionately, caught in a moment of conflicting emotions.

Kurt Cobain stepped out of the car and headed towards the terminal entrance. As the automatic doors slid open, he passed through them swiftly, disappearing into the busy terminal.

Another bad decision. Cortney thought to herself.

Cortney watched silently from her car, parked nearby. Her expression conflicted, she hesitated for a moment, then started the engine and drove away into the night, leaving the airport behind.

***

Kurt Fenstad's car cruised along the bustling 405 Freeway, heading from the Westside towards the valley under the clear Los Angeles sky.

Kurt Fenstad reached over and flicked on the radio. The morning show's gentle chatter was suddenly interrupted by a serious voice.

We have some sad news to announce today. The lead singer of Nirvana, Kurt Cobain, killed himself by gunshot wound to his head. Kurt Cobain is dead at the age of 27.

Cortney's hand moved quickly to the radio dial, shutting off the broadcast. She stared out of the car window with thoughts that were heavy and unreadable.

Chapter 11:
Part 1
Was I Ever Married?

In the depths of memories, vows spoken,
now silent

Kurt Fenstad's car entered the television studio parking lot. Cortney exited quickly, slamming the door behind her. She and Kurt headed toward the audition office. Both of them sat in the waiting room, the soft tapping of the receptionist's keyboard and the occasional ring of the phone created a subdued background noise. Just then, the phone rang, breaking the silence.

"Hi, Marta. OK, I'll send her in," the receptionist said, then looked at Cortney. "Cortney?"

"Yes," Cortney replied, standing up.

"Marta Kauffman will see you now," the receptionist informed her.

Cortney walked through the office door, leaving Kurt behind. He picked up a magazine and started reading an article about Bill and Melinda Gates, their smiling faces framed by a picture of their daughter.

Just after a short while, Cortney came running out of the office with tears flowing down her face. Marta Kauffman followed her into the waiting room with a look of confusion on her face.

"I don't know what got into her. This is a comedy," Marta said, shaking her head.

Kurt put down the magazine and stood up. "Cortney's mom had Munchausen Syndrome by Proxy. She has these crying fits because of it," he explained.

Marta looked at Cortney with a softer expression. "I want you to come back next week when you are feeling better," she said kindly.

***

The next day, Cortney stood in line holding a stack of papers tightly in her hands, inside the bustling Screen Actors Guild office. The space was filled with the low murmur of conversations and the clatter of a keyboard. When it was her turn, she approached the receptionist with a determined look on her face

"I'd like to withdraw from the union," Cortney said in a steady voice despite the gravity of her request.

The receptionist, a middle-aged woman, looked up from her computer and frowned slightly. "Oh, no, you can't," she replied gently. "You can't stop paying your dues. Once you're in the union, you're always in the union."

Cortney sighed and her shoulders slumped as she absorbed the information. The receptionist's words lingered in her mind, reminding her of the inescapable ties to the industry. She nodded slowly and turned away from the desk, feeling the weight of her decision press down on her.

***

One sunny day, Cortney, and Brad Pitt were enjoying their lunch at Renee's Courtyard Restaurant, talking about this and that. Just then, their waitress Jennifer Aniston, 25, moved around the busy courtyard with a friendly smile.

"You're the controller of my destiny. Whatever you tell me to do, I'll do," Brad said, looking earnestly at Cortney.

"Where's our waitress?" Cortney asked, scanning the area. "What do you mean 'you'll do anything'?"

Jennifer Aniston approached the table, flipping her hair with ease.

"There you are," Cortney said. "Are you an actress?"

"Why, yes I am," Jennifer replied, flipping her hair again.

"Good, because you're a horrible waitress. I'll have another glass of Chardonnay," Cortney said dismissively.

Jennifer walked away, and Cortney turned back to Brad. "You should marry the waitress. She obviously won't be able to support herself waiting tables."

"Why don't you marry?" Brad asked with

curiosity in his voice.

"Oh, no, I can't get married. If I do, I must marry an African. I can only have one child and must marry after the baby is born," Cortney replied nonchalantly.

"Who told you this?" Brad inquired with a frown.

"I met this Saudi Arabian diplomat, who told me that I was Jackie O's secret daughter and that six weeks after my wedding, there will be two planes into the World Trade Center. A missile would hit the Pentagon and the White House. I begged they spare the White House," Cortney explained.

"You shouldn't tell people that you are a Kennedy. What about this diplomat? Have you met him before?" Brad asked as concern crept into his voice.

"His voice sounded familiar. I grew up in a Mormon foster home, and it sounded like the owner of the Mormon Church who used to call my parents. At least, that's what I remember. I could be wrong," Cortney said as Jennifer Aniston returned with Cortney's wine.

"Why not tell people I'm a Kennedy?" Cortney continued. "Don't you think leaders of other countries know that I exist? Everything is said for a reason at the time they are said. You see, the Administration is a corporation. You've got a President and a Treasury or a President and Attorney General. JFK and the Kennedy family were creating a Monarchy. He was printing his own money six weeks before his murder. You see, FDR started our credit system with our social security benefits. He borrowed on nine different crops, but not marijuana, which once made our nation rich. Anyway, everything was made out of hemp before prohibition. Also, Joseph Kennedy, my supposed grandfather, changed from a Republican to a Democrat to work for FDR and wrote the Security Exchange Commission rules. What I am saying is we are stock. Our birth certificate is our receipt of bonds traded on Wall Street. We are not created equal. The Kennedys were killed because of their bastard children carrying on their social security bond that the government keeps, especially if the children are raised in a foster home, like me and Marilyn."

"Who is Marilyn's parents?" Brad asked out of intrigue.

"Her mother was Gladys something or another, and she worked for RKO Studios owned by Howard Hughes, Marilyn's biological father. Howard Hughes left his fortune to the Mormons. The Mormons and the government are fighting over it even to this day. And I was raised Mormon, where my adoption records are sealed for 100 years if I'm adopted. It really is a cult," Cortney explained.

"So, what do you get out of this deal of not getting married?" Brad asked.

"I begged for it not to happen, but this Golem told me it was inevitable. So, I asked for the legalization of pot," Cortney replied.

"That's a good deal, I guess, if you have to make one. What's his name? Golem?" Brad asked.

"Yeah, I think so. For the Golan Heights in Israel. Golan is a sand monster that protected Israel from an air raid. Did you know that Holocaust victims struck a deal to get money on 6 million dead Jews? It is not mathematically possible that, that many people died in the time period of World War II. It's draining our credit system, which is Social Security. John McCloy made the deal and was directly involved with the JFK cover-up. If my mother had me as First Lady that would make me a queen. I learned that in high school," Cortney said.

"Learned what?" Brad asked in confusion.

"If the First Lady gives birth in office, our government changes to a Monarchy," Cortney explained.

"Have you been married before?" Brad asked, still processing everything.

"Not that I remember," Cortney replied.

In the midst of her memories, Cortney found herself transported back to a busy day at Garden Grove Courthouse. Alongside her was Gino Zammit, then 28, a man with a birth certificate from Malta. They stood in line together, approaching the cashier with a mix of determination and uncertainty. Cortney's mind raced, trying hard to recall if she had been married to Gino or merely sponsoring him at that time. Each handed over their respective birth certificates, a pivotal moment that seemed both vivid and distant in her mind's eye.

"Sign any name," Gino suggested to Cortney with a casual smile.

"Any name? Okay," Cortney replied with uncertainty.

Later that day, at a quaint Newport Beach restaurant, Cortney and Gino settled into their seats just as the waitress approached their table.

"I love your outfit," the waitress complimented Cortney.

"Thank you. I made it," Cortney responded a sense of pride.

"Are you a designer?" the waitress inquired curiously.

"I go to Los Angeles Trade Tech for fashion design. I made it for my wedding day," Cortney explained.

"Come to think of it, I may have married Gino Zammit to keep him in the country. No. I was sponsoring him. At least, I don't think I married him," Cortney reflected aloud, coming back to the present.

"Italian?" Brad Pitt asked, seeking clarification.

"Maltese. My Sicilian foster father introduced us," Cortney clarified.

"What does he do?" Brad inquired further.

"He's an actor, by my recommendation. I had dreamed of being a Hollywood super couple, but I withdrew from SAG. Did you know that once you are in the union, you are always in the union?" Cortney mused, shaking her head slightly.

"How does this Gino make a living?" Brad queried, shifting the conversation.

"He grows pot in Vegas and owns Café Croissant on the Venice Beach boardwalk, where I met him, and the reason I moved to L.A.," Cortney explained.

"What else did this Golem instruct you to do?"

"Said something about Canadian twins and an Orlando," Cortney replied.

"Orlando the place or Orlando the person?" Brad sought clarification.

"I don't know, but I'll figure it out. I always do," Cortney affirmed with determination.

"I'll be back," Brad Pitt said, excusing himself to enter the restaurant just as Jennifer Aniston arrived with the check.

"You get this one. I'll pick up the next check," Brad remarked casually before heading inside.

Cortney watched him go, her thoughts wandering as Jennifer Aniston placed the bill on their table and followed Brad inside.

Well, that's the last time I ever go to lunch with him, Cortney thought to herself, reaching into her purse to leave enough cash for the bill, including a two-cent tip.

Chapter 11:
Part 2
Footsteps in Passing

Each meeting, a verse in life's unfolding poem.

12 Years Later...

The hustle and bustle of O.R. Tambo International Airport was in full swing. Bill Gates, now 51, stood in the American passport line, a composed and familiar figure among the travelers. At the back of the line was Cortney Page, 41, her appearance drastically changed over the years. She wore long hair extensions, a low-cut top, and tight jeans. With enhanced lips and boobs, she looked remarkably like Anna Nicole Smith.

Bill Gates spotted Cortney from a distance and waved over a security guard. After a brief exchange, the guard walked towards Cortney.

"Follow me," the security guard instructed.

Cortney, slightly taken aback, complied. She followed the guard as he led her to where Bill Gates stood in the passport line.

As she walked, Cortney's thoughts began to swirl. *Do I know him? He looks awfully familiar, she thought to herself,* trying to place the man who seemed so intent on meeting her.

***

At the Reggae on the River festival, a laid-back event where music filled the air and people lounged by the water, Cortney, 35, was forcibly sat down on a beach chair by the river next to two men and Bill Gates, then 45. Bill Gates casually munched on a bag of sunflower seeds in a calm and unassuming way.

"Do I know you? You look awfully familiar," Cortney asked, as her eyes narrowed in confusion.

"He's your husband." One of the men responded.

"Is that true?" Cortney turned to Bill, searching for recognition in his blank stare.

"Tell him everything you know." The man urged.

Cortney took a deep breath, her voice steady. "The beast is in Israel, and we need to change the binary code."

"Cortney, I want you to go swim over to that bush. You heard me. Go. Go on. Go." The man then directed her with a firm tone.

With a perfect butt in a G-string bikini, Cortney got up and swam towards the bush, with confident and swift strokes. She swam underwater, reaching the bush where Brad Pitt stood, holding a gun and shaking in fear.

"Someone is going to die today," Brad Pitt said in a trembling voice. "Either that man sitting over there that has 10,000 employees or you."

"Well, I guess it's a good day to die." Cortney said in an unbothered way as she met his gaze.

As she dove into the river and swam back to the men and Bill Gates. Suddenly, Brad caught her, his grip tightening as he forcibly held her underwater. Panic surged through her as she struggled, his hands pressing down on her. Through the rippling water, she saw the sun, its light distorted and wavering above.

***

Cortney walked into the private TV room of the Starlight Nightclub. The dim lighting cast a mysterious glow, and as she stepped inside, Brandon Lee turned around to face her.

"You're the prophecy," Cortney said, her voice filled with awe and certainty.

"So are you," Brandon Lee replied calmly as his eyes met hers.

On the television screen, a strange scene played out. Cortney was shown given a grass-like straw to breathe through, pretending to be dead. The tension in the room was evident. Suddenly, Brad grabbed her from behind, his breath warm against her ear as he whispered. "Go spit on Bill, or I'll shoot you. Do you understand me?" Brad's voice was low and menacing.

Cortney nodded as her heart pounded. She knew she had no choice. Emerging from the water, she made her way to Bill Gates. Without hesitation, she spat on him and then skipped away. Around her, hundreds of people were stunned in silence, the abrupt scene unfolding before their eyes left their mouths open in shock.

***

Back at the airport, Cortney stood nervously by Bill Gates in the passport line, glancing around at the bustling terminal.

"I'm Bill," Bill Gates said, turning to her with a polite smile.

"Nice to meet you, Bill. I'm Glossy," she replied.

"Are you traveling for business or pleasure?" he asked in a casual tone.

"I'm traveling with my husband. We're visiting my in-laws and staying at their newly built mansion on the beach in Kommetjie. It's taken four years to build, and my husband helped with the construction. We have a modern marriage. We don't live together; we take vacations with each other. I live in Lake Arrowhead, and he lives in L.A. We see each other on the weekends when he's in the States. And you?" she explained in a swift manner.

"How big is your in-laws' house?" Bill inquired out of curiosity.

"This house is six thousand square feet," Cortney replied.

"My house is ten thousand square feet," Bill stated matter-of-factly.

"Your wife is a lucky woman," Cortney commented with admiration in her voice.

"I haven't lived with my wife for over ten years," Bill confessed.

"So, you have a modern marriage like me, where we don't live with our spouses," Cortney noted.

"Lake Arrowhead is a lot like Seattle," Bill remarked, nodding thoughtfully.

"That's what I always say," Cortney agreed with a small smile forming.

"Why did you move to Seattle?" Bill asked, his questions aimed at sparking her memory, because deep down, he held a faint hope that she might still remember him.

"To catch the Green River Killer. I heard they caught the guy," Cortney replied.

"What do you do?" Bill asked, shifting the conversation.

"I sell time for a living. I get paid per minute to talk on the phone as a life coach," Cortney explained.

"When did you get married?" Bill inquired.

"Six weeks before 9/11," Cortney replied.

As Bill glanced at Cortney beside him, a fleeting memory surged through his mind — the time he had spent with her, giving advice and sharing moments of pleasure. It was a surreal juxtaposition.

Bill Gates, 42, and Cortney, 32, sat close together on a plush loveseat in the luxurious Bellagio Hotel suite. Across from them, three imposing Italian mobsters occupied chairs, their demeanor serious and watchful.

"Are you two married?" Nunzio Desantis, one of the three men asked.

"No, because six weeks after I marry, two planes fly into the World Trade Center. A missile didn't hit the Pentagon and the White House. That hasn't happened, so I'm not married." Cortney explained.

***

Back to present, Bill and Cortney continue their conversation at the airport.

"What do your in-laws do for a living?" Bill asked.

"My father-in-law runs the media in the whole of South Africa. Well, that's what they say. He's on the Board of Independent Newspapers and is Tony O'Reilly's right hand man. Tony O'Reilly runs BBC media." Cortney explained intently.

"I should have given you money." Bill replied.

***

Cortney, 32, and Bill Gates, 42, made out in the Jacuzzi at a swimming pool in Bellagio Hotel.

THE GATES OF NIRVANA'S PIT

Cortney went under water, and Bill's eyes rolled to the back of his head. She came up for air, turned around, and sat on his lap.

"You know we could be arrested for this." Bill said in a seductive tone.

"Maybe you can. But I have diplomatic immunity." Cortney replied with mischief.

They continued to passionately kiss each other. They made love in every part of the hotel, not leaving any opportunity at hand.

Cortney held a towel, and she and Bill Gates had sex in the elevator. The elevator door opened, and people glared in shock. After a brief awkward moment the door closed.

Back in the room, Cortney stood naked with her butt pressed up against the window as Bill Gates had sex with her standing up.

After their wild adventures in the hotel, Cortney soaked herself in a relaxing bubble bath when Bill Gates entered, taking a seat on the toilet.

"If I got you pregnant, would you keep the baby? I ask because I paid for your boyfriend's abortion." Bill inquired out of the blue.

"I don't know what you're talking about," Cortney replied, puzzled. "Who are you, anyway? Have we met before? Because all I know is I promised Nunzio DeSantis I'd give you the best time of your life."

Bill Gates sighed, running a hand through his

hair. "How did you meet Nunzio?"

"From the Peninsula Hotel in Beverly Hills. My friend, Jenna King, is a Madonna impersonator for 'Legends.' She set up a meeting with the producer, and Nunzio sent a drink over to me. That's my story, and I'm sticking to it." She said in a firm tone.

Cortney submerged herself in the water, avoiding his gaze, as Bill Gates flushed the toilet and sat down.

In the checkout line, Cortney and Bill Gates kissed and held hands.

"Will you gift me some cash?" Cortney asked.

Bill Gates took out his wallet and handed her his business card. "Call me. We'll talk about millions."

They kissed again passionately. Cortney walked away with tears streaming down her face, and defiantly threw the business card into a nearby trash can.

***

A cab rolled to a stop, and Cortney stepped out onto the deserted lot of the Countryland abandoned hotel.

"Are you sure this is where your meeting is?" the Cab Driver asked, eyeing the dilapidated building.

"I'm meeting with the owners to talk about

costumes and interior design ideas," Cortney replied confidently.

"The mob owns this building, and they're tearing it down, is what I've heard," the Cab Driver warned.

"Well, I'm here, so I might as well go in and see what they want," Cortney shrugged, heading towards the Countryland Hotel.

Inside the cab, the driver dialed dispatch.

"This is dispatch," came the voice on the other end.

"Yeah, can you send the police to the Countryland Hotel?" the Cab Driver requested urgently. "I just dropped off a girl who says she's there to decorate, but it's scheduled to be demolished."

The dispatcher acknowledged the request as the cab driver watched Cortney disappear through the hotel's doors, concerned for her safety amidst the looming demolition.

Inside, Nunzio, Joey, and Cortney navigated through the dusty hallways of the abandoned hotel towards a large corral room that they entered cautiously.

"Is this where there will be the donkey shows?" Cortney asked nervously, scanning the room.

Joey suddenly turned towards her, brandishing a gun.

"You don't want to kill me, Joey," Cortney pleaded. "Nunzio, stop him. You'll be caught, Joey, and go back to prison for the rest of your life. Whatever you're being paid, I'll double it."

Before Joey could react, the doors burst open, flooding the room with light as a dozen police officers stormed in, guns drawn. Joey quickly concealed his weapon.

"Las Vegas P.D.!" one of the officers announced firmly.

Cortney turned towards them with relief.

"Hello officers, we were just having a business meeting," she explained calmly, trying to compose herself amidst the tension.

The officers surveyed the scene cautiously, assessing the situation before addressing Cortney and the men with her.

***

Back to the present, Cortney and Bill Gates approached the immigration officer's desk with their passports in hand.

"Were you the one that sent me a drink on my wedding day?" Cortney asked casually as they waited.

"Someone sent you a drink on your wedding day?" Bill Gates looked puzzled.

"Yeah, I guess it wasn't you," Cortney replied, shaking her head.

The immigration officer gestured for Cortney to step forward.

"Do you have a small dog?" Bill Gates queried before she moved away.

"No. I've got a 60-pound dog. He's saved my life a few times," Cortney answered with a smile.

"Do you drink?" Bill Gates glanced at her thoughtfully.

"Buds and Suds," she replied, stepping up to the immigration desk. "I'm next."

"On a scale from 1 to 10, where are you with happiness?" Bill Gates continued in a curious voice.

"An 8, but there's always room for improvement," Cortney said warmly. "Well, it was really nice meeting you, Bill. Have a good trip. Bye."

Cortney turned to the immigration officer, who promptly addressed her.

"Here for pleasure or business?" the officer inquired.

"Pleasure," Cortney confirmed, ready to continue her journey.

"Please sign these forms," the immigration officer instructed, handing her paperwork.

"What am I signing?" Cortney asked, taking a look at the documents.

"Documents for the man standing in line

behind you," the officer explained.

Cortney turned, expecting to see Bill Gates, but he had disappeared. She signed the paperwork and proceeded through the line. On the other side, she spotted her South African husband, 42, resembling Jude Law dressed as a biker with long dark curly hair. They embraced each other and kissed warmly.

"Who were you talking to?" he asked, glancing back towards where they had come from.

"Some guy named Bill," Cortney replied with a wistful smile on her face. "The strange thing is, it seemed like he knew me. Where's Emma Lee?" Cortney asked excitedly.

Her husband pointed towards a 5-year-old blonde little girl, who was gazing out the window at the planes with wide eyes.

Cortney, her husband, and Emma Lee continued through the airport, hand in hand, surrounded by the sounds of travelers and the sights of departure boards and bustling crowds.

As they walked, Cortney's thoughts drifted, narrating softly to herself.

A part of me wanted to throw my arms around Bill like he was an old friend. He's another familiar stranger. Maybe next time when our paths cross? If not in this life, in the next. This life has been only to the gates of Nirvana's pit.

For anyone curious, Cortney Page is still happily married, living in Lake Arrowhead, California.